MAYHEM

OTHER BOOKS BY SISSELA BOK

Lying: Moral Choice in Public and Private Life
Secrets: On the Ethics of Concealment and Revelation
A Strategy For Peace: Human Values and the Threat of War
Alva Myrdal: A Daughter's Memoir
Common Values

MAYHEM

violence as public entertainment

SISSELA BOK

A MERLOYD LAWRENCE BOOK

PERSEUS BOOKS

Reading, Massachusetts

Library of Congress Cataloging-in-Publication Data

Bok, Sissela.
    Mayhem : violence as public entertainment / Sissela Bok.
       p.   cm.
    "A Merloyd Lawrence book."
    Includes bibliographical references and index.
    ISBN 0-201-48979-1
    1. Violence in mass media.   I. Title.
  P96.V5B65   1998
  303.6—dc21   97-48620
                                            CIP

Perseus Books is a member of the Perseus Books Group

Jacket design by Suzanne Heiser
Text design by Karen Savary
Set in 11.5-point Weiss by Pagesetters, Inc., Brattleboro, VT

2 3 4 5 6 7 8 9–MA–0201009998
Second printing, July 1998

Find us on the World Wide Web at
http://www.aw.com/gb/

For Cameron

CONTENTS

MAYHEM

INTRODUCTION

*The true hero, the true subject, the center of the Iliad is force. Force
employed by man, force that enslaves man, force behind which
man's flesh shrinks away. In this work, at all times, the human
spirit is shown as modified by its relations with force, as swept
away, blinded, by the very force it imagined it could handle, as
deformed by the weight of the force it submits to.*

SIMONE WEIL, *THE ILIAD OR THE POEM OF FORCE*[1]

In the lowland rainforest of south-central New Guinea lives a tribe of
about 450 persons, the Gebusi. Few societies go so far in repudiating
all expressions of anger and violence. Anthropologist Bruce Knauft has
described the Gebusi stress on kindliness, mutual deference, communal sharing, and cooperation, and their affectionate practices of child-
rearing:

> The primary cultural value instilled in young children is "good
> company" (*kog-wa-yay*). This term is also used by the Gebusi to
> describe their customs and way of life as a whole. The
> component concepts of this term—togetherness, casual talk,
> and exuberant humor—are the most immediate and striking

dimensions of Gebusi social life. The opposite, negatively valued trait, is *gof*, which connotes anger, hardness, and violence.[2]

Even in their entertainments, the Gebusi allow only the mildest portrayals of violence. Communal feasts are preceded by carefully staged displays of ritual antagonism between members of different groups, but before severe physical harm is inflicted, neutral parties "quickly interpose themselves between the opposing sides, and all persons proceed to snap fingers in peace [like shaking hands] and enter the longhouse for a night of feasting and celebrating."[3]

For anyone who views our own levels of violent conduct with dismay, such peaceful practices present an appealing contrast. It is the more surprising, then, to learn that this Gebusi society, so rejecting of brutality and unkindness, has one of the highest known homicide rates yet recorded—about forty times the U.S. rate.[4] Almost a third of all adult Gebusi deaths result from killing. The victims are most often persons whom villagers suspect of having used sorcery to make a fellow Gebusi fall ill and die. Such killings are quickly hushed up. Since there are no legal or other authorities in this thoroughly egalitarian society, there is no way to bring perpetrators to trial or punish them—they are simply executed by consensual agreement. After the killing, however, the entire community does all it can to avoid dwelling on the deadly event and to return to the usual peaceful patterns of "good company." Because of the small size of the Gebusi population, considerable time may elapse between one such killing and the next— one reason why visiting anthropologists have often idealized such societies as remarkably nonviolent.

The very stress, among the Gebusi, on avoiding violence in ritual performance, in entertainment, and in open discussion makes it harder for them to cope with the threat of killing once it arises. But while acknowledging the realities of violence by such means is indispensable for coming to terms with them, it cannot suffice. In most societies, the very practices of routinized aggression in games, spectacles, and rituals of sacrifice that allow for expressions of anger and hostility also serve to shield people against full confrontation with the role of violence in their midst.[5]

The United States has the highest levels of homicide of any advanced industrial democracy in the world. Like the Gebusi, we have failed to come to grips with the cultural aspects of violence in our society; but not for lack of representation of any of its facets in art and entertainment. On the contrary: We can draw on religious and philosophical traditions and on works of literature and art to explore the nature of violence; and we have introduced forms and amounts of media violence beyond anything achieved in other countries. What has been lacking, rather, is a probing society-wide discussion of violence in society and its links with cultural life, including all forms of entertainment. Few doubt that the present massive exposure to graphic acts of violence has a significant impact on those who experience it. But although social scientists and child advocates have been exploring the effects of such exposure for decades, it is only in recent years that a groundswell of concern, both at home and abroad, has generated a wide-ranging public debate about possible effects and how we might best respond.

In this book, I hope to contribute to this growing debate, with special focus on works produced, marketed, and consumed as *entertainment violence*, for pleasure, excitement, thrill. Do they contribute to callousness and violent crime, as large majorities of Americans tell pollsters, or do they merely provide harmless amusement?[6] In either case, might such works also help viewers confront and deal with violence in real life, perhaps informing them better or satisfying some deep-seated need that might otherwise find more brutal expression? Is it alarmist or merely sensible to ask about what happens to the souls of children nurtured, as in no past society, on images of rape, torture, bombings, and massacre that are channeled into their homes from infancy? These questions, in turn, raise larger ones about the media, entertainment, and violent crime in contemporary societies; about the mass marketing of violence as sexy and of sexuality as violent; about human vulnerability and resilience; and about how to learn to deal with the reality as well as the fantasy of violence.

There is, to be sure, nothing new about the attraction of violence in its own right. Crowds in many societies have watched hangings and other public executions with awe and relish. People have thrilled since the beginning of time to hearing horror stories and war epics, and to viewing combat between every kind of living being that could be induced or compelled to fight in front of spectators, from cocks to cobras, from mongooses to human beings. But it is only in the last five decades that it has become possible for people to tune in to violent programming with graphic immediacy on home screens at all hours of the day and night; and only in the past few decades that America's entertainment industry has grown into one of our country's largest producers and exporters, targeting children as an especially lucrative market for violent programming.[7]

By now, television brings into most homes news reports of rape, torture, and murder worldwide, rebroadcasting the most brutal scenes such as the Rodney King beating or the Oklahoma City bombing over and over until they become burned into the mind's eye. In some cities what has been called the "Mayhem Index"—the percentage of local news reporting that deals with violent topics such as crime, war, terrorism, and disaster—reaches levels over 75 percent. And during the 1990s, while the homicide rate dropped in the United States, network evening news coverage of murder escalated: between 1993 and 1996, it soared by an average of 721 percent, compared with the three previous years.[8]

Images of violence are then reflected, repeated, and echoed in endless variations through the lens of entertainment violence, suffusing movie and TV screens, filling the airwaves, recounted in best-selling novels. In interactive games marketed to children and young people, participants are rewarded for shooting, eviscerating, and strangling victims. And the "splatter and gore" films that are widely available on cable and video variously provide, for the enjoyment of viewers, such scenes as the crushing of skulls and the tearing out of hearts from living persons and rotting corpses.

As we consider these facts, the temptation is strong to avert our eyes, to close off questioning, and to assume that it is either unnecessary or too difficult to probe deeply, let alone shape an adequate response.[9] The sense of helplessness that so many experience with respect to media violence is heightened when dismissive claims appear to foreclose further exploration. While such claims bring out points worth making, they are taken too far when used to foreshorten the debate about media violence. In so doing, they impede each of four crucial phases of any moral response: they thwart efforts to strive for the fullest *perception* of what is at issue, to engage in the fairest *deliberation* in the light of the available evidence and possible counterarguments, to seek to arrive at the most justifiable *choice*, and to *implement* that choice to the best of one's ability. In each phase, it is often easiest to opt for premature closure, forgoing efforts at the fullest perception and deliberation and settling for uncritical acceptance of dismissive rhetoric.

1. One common argument rejects public concern over media violence as one more way to avoid facing up to the real causes of societal violence. Why blame the media when so much more violence is caused by family breakdown, the availability of firearms, substance abuse and deep strains of violence in our culture? Media violence offers an especially tempting scapegoat, "much easier to attack," in the words of television director Michael Mann, "than the imponderables of why there's so much violence in this culture."[10]

Such challenges are valuable insofar as they caution against exclusive focus on media violence, or indeed on guns or drugs or any single factor. There is clearly good reason to address the role of each and every one. To concentrate only on media violence, in an effort to understand societal violence more generally, would be not only mistaken but dangerous. But it would be equally misguided to allow such claims to block any concern with media violence or with any other risk factor until all the other problems contributing to societal violence have been adequately dealt with. Complex, multidimensional human problems cannot be effectively addressed in this manner. Take heart disease: No one maintains that, just because a number of risk factors such as smoking and heredity and cholesterol contribute to the prevalence of this disease, we should focus on no single one of them or on the ways in which they interact. Instead, research and public health policy must continue to take each one into account, including those of lesser magnitude. So long as media violence is not seen as the only contributing factor, moreover, the claim that paying attention to it represents "an easy way out" is beside the point. Why *not* address the easier as well as the harder aspects of a problem?

2. One of the quickest ways to short-circuit serious reflection about any form of violence is to insist that it is impossible to define it specifically enough for policy debates.[11] After all, some people define "violence" so broadly as to include all injustice, even as others have claimed that all fiction is lying, all property theft, all sexual intercourse rape.[12] If people can't even agree on how to define "violence," then how can they go on to discuss what to do about it? People surely do define it in different ways; but if we waited to debate almost any complex issue until doubts and disagreements about definitions were resolved, we would have little left to discuss. The philosopher John Searle has pointed out that "one of the most important insights of recent work in the philosophy of language [has been that] most non-technical concepts in ordinary language lack absolutely strict rules" according to which one can definitely state when they do and do not apply.[13] This is as true of concepts such as "promising" or "lying" as of "violence." All can be conceived either more broadly or more narrowly. All present problems of line-drawing.[14] Yet with respect to none would it make sense to postpone analysis and debate until complete agreement on definitions has been reached.

For purposes of starting the debate about what should count as media violence, what is needed is to begin by agreeing on some baseline minimal definition. Consider the Oxford English Dictionary's core definition of "violence" as "the exercise of physical force so as to inflict injury or damage to persons or property."[15] It is hard to think of anyone whose preferred definition would not cover at least such injury. "Media violence" could then be defined at least as the conveying or portrayal of such exercises of force in the press or on the radio or the screen. And "entertainment violence" could likewise be defined at least to include forms of media violence offered as entertainment.

With such a basis, it becomes possible to ask whether the relevant definition of "violence" should include further distinctions: those, for instance between harm done to others and to oneself, as in self-mutilation or suicide; between harm that is unwanted by the recipient and desired harm, as by penitents or masochists; and between unlawful or unauthorized harm and harm inflicted in accordance with laws of the particular society in which it takes place, such as hangings or electrocutions.[16] Exploring such distinctions and the differing definitions of violence on which they rely helps us to understand violence better and to deal with it more cogently. But when it comes to what is to count as media violence, it turns out that some such distinctions matter more than others. For example, most people will regard homicide and suicide by gunshot, if committed on the screen, as equally violent. As for small children, they cannot draw such distinctions at all. A three- or four-year-old is unlikely, in viewing a series of killings, to sort out the degree to which they are intentional, or to react differently depending on whether the killings are unlawful or authorized.

3. A third argument holds that our society is so inherently violent that debates about media violence are largely beside the point. H. Rap Brown's claim, in 1967, that "violence is as American as cherry pie" has entered the vernacular.[17] How can those who wish to address the problem be other than discouraged, once they take into account our country's history of slavery, frontier violence, labor strife, racial conflict, crime, and warfare? Who could possibly imagine that policies with respect to media

violence could have much effect on attitudes so ingrained in our national psyche? For those especially given to self-flagellation, D. H. Lawrence's oft-quoted assertion that "the essential American soul is hard, stoic, isolate, and a killer" only confirms their view that little can be done about violence of any kind in our society.

In recent decades, many have further concluded that the United States is not only inherently violent but uniquely so. Ask any group of people to name the three societies in the world with the highest measured levels of homicide, and chances are that America will top the list. During the years when I worked on this book, I posed this question to people at gatherings both at home and abroad. Invariably, most took for granted that the United States is among the most violent countries on earth, if not the most violent of them all.[18] Foreign policy experts, military strategists, and peace activists showed no greater hesitation in this respect than others. Young and old, liberal and conservative, religious and agnostic—all were equally startled at being told that they were wrong: that many developing societies have homicide rates several times that of the United States; and that in 1995, the latest available homicide statistics showed Colombia, South Africa, and Russia to be the three countries in the lead.[19]

True, the United States does have the highest rate of homicide among advanced industrial democracies—in 1996, about 7.4 per 100,000 persons.[20] By 1962, the U.S. homicide rate had fallen from 6.9 per 100,000 in 1946 to 4.5 per 100,000, a level not far above that of other advanced industrial democracies. Thereafter, the levels began a prolonged upward move to reach 9.4 per 100,000 in 1972.[21] Cresting in the early 1980s, then resuming its climb after a downward turn, the U.S. rate topped 10 per 100,000 in 1991, only to begin a sharp downturn again in the 1990s. These fluctuations remind us that there is nothing immutable about levels of violence in America.

Just as "slavery is as American as cherry pie" might have seemed to some all too accurate a characterization of part of

American society in 1850, it would have been similarly inadequate as a reason for contending that slavery could not be overcome. Invoking perennial American patterns of violence helps obscure inquiry into explanations for present levels of violence and into contributing factors and possible remedies. Such claims are singularly inappropriate, moreover, when advanced in connection with TV violence, which is precisely not as perennially American as cherry pie: it is only five decades since a few American households acquired their first television sets.

4. A last form of overhasty dismissal holds that the time to provide a meaningful societal response to media violence has passed, now that so many new means of transmitting violent material are becoming available. If America could not formulate adequate policies before the era of cable, video, and the Internet, why should anyone imagine that the task will be easier in the future? This argument points to a valid problem. But it would be premature to abandon the search for solutions merely on that ground. After all, air and water pollution, too, spring from increasingly numerous sources and spread in ways that make them difficult to regulate, yet few people propose, on that ground, that we should give up on collective measures to deal with them.[22] On the contrary, the increasing number of channels and the growth of the new media may render it more urgent than ever to ask whether it is necessary to take steps to guard against the flow of media violence before it becomes still more difficult to do so.

Two kinds of help exist now, moreover, that were not available in the past. First of all, data from other countries are increasingly available. Censorship in theocracies and secular dictatorships underscores the reasons for not moving in that direction. Many democracies, including England, France, Australia, Norway, Sweden, and Canada, have engaged in articulate public debates about media violence, and some have developed policies to cut back substantially on the flood of violence that would otherwise be reaching young children. Just as American research and case materials have been helpful to the national debates in these countries, so we in turn can learn a great deal from these debates and from international conferences where new approaches are increasingly discussed.[23]

A second type of help not formerly available resides in some of the new technologies themselves. Even as they have made possible the channeling of violent entertainment into every home, they are also facilitating the emergence of a multitude of alternatives to its consumption, as well as new ways for individuals to exercise choice for themselves and their children. At the very least, therefore, it would be premature to foreclose examining the impact of media violence and the possibilities for creative responses. This book is devoted to such an exploration.

■   ■   ■

In Part One, "The Paradox of Entertainment Violence," I take up the most spectacular displays of entertainment violence in history—the gladiatorial games in ancient Rome—to examine the hold that violence can come to have on the emotions of an entire population and to ask what relevance their experience might have for our present debates. Unlike the Gebusi, the Romans openly celebrated violence, but they, too, were expert at deflecting the need to understand its role in their lives. It is the special allure of violence for the Romans that raises most sharply the question of moral conflict, even paradox. Then as now, some found the notion that violence should be entertaining utterly self-contradictory, much like the notion of a "kindly rapist" or a "two-sided triangle"; others viewed it as unproblematic and simply confirming the perennial human delight in mayhem.

While Americans have no precise equivalents to the levels of real-life public carnage that so delighted the Romans, we may be able to learn from their experience and from the role of the political and commercial interests that stood to gain from promoting the public's passion for the games. Is it always possible to distinguish what St. Augustine called the "stabbing of the soul" of persons addicted to the slaughter in the Roman circuses and amphitheaters from the *catharsis* possible through works such as the *Iliad* and the tragedies of Sophocles? And how might we draw such distinctions with regard to contemporary films, video games, and television programming?

Part Two, "The Impact of Media Violence," considers the findings of current research. In what sense, if any, does the media's focus on carnage and crime inure us to real-life violence? Does it affect viewers for the worse, or does it have salutary effects, such as providing an outlet for venting aggression vicariously, perhaps even teaching them how to guard better against actual violence? Four possible negative effects have been most frequently studied: increased fearfulness, progressive desensitization, greater appetite for more frequent and more violent programming, and higher levels of aggression. Of these, the first two are most often linked to heavy exposure to media violence generally, including documentaries and newscasts; the latter two are associated with the consumption of entertainment violence in particular. Part II also explores the effects of media violence on young children's moral development before they have learned to tell the difference between what happens on the screen and in real life. Under what conditions can such experience contribute to a psychological "failure to thrive," analogous to the nutritional failure to thrive diagnosed in severely deprived or malnourished babies and small children?

Part Three, "Censorship," addresses the dilemma between unfettered violent programming and government control over what is spoken, written, and performed. We can't wipe violence off the screen, let alone out of our culture. Must we therefore conclude that no meaningful policy change is possible short of censorship? I examine this question against the background of centuries of controversy. Long after the fall of Rome, concern with "spectacles" in Europe culminated in a debate about whether to outlaw all theatrical productions, a debate that engaged Enlightenment figures such as Rousseau, Voltaire, and d'Alembert. More recently, similar tensions have arisen in Iran, Singapore, and a number of other countries attempting to restrict access to the Internet. In our own society, journalists and legal scholars are only beginning to address the hardest questions about the production, dissemination, and consumption of media violence.

Part Four, "Opportunities," examines ways for families, communities, and public policymakers to guard against the effects of entertainment violence without resorting to official censorship. I aim, in this final part, to challenge the helplessness that so many now experience with respect to media and especially entertainment violence: a helplessness that reflects a deeper unrest about families and cultures, about the kind of society ours is becoming, and about our responsibilities to one another, to our children, and to ourselves. I argue that there is no reason to feel impotent, no excuse to opt out. The factors entering into the sense of paradox and of moral and empirical dilemma are, when examined, far from immobilizing. Beyond these barriers, opportunities for imaginative responses abound.

PART ONE
the paradox of entertainment violence

The people that once bestowed commands, consulships,
legions, and all else, now concerns itself no more, and longs
eagerly for just two things—bread and circuses!

JUVENAL, SATIRES[1]

Maybe we need the catharsis of blood-letting and
decapitation, like the Ancient Romans needed it, as ritual,
but not real like the Roman Circus.   MARTIN SCORSESE[2]

FEASTS OF
VIOLENCE

No people before or since have so reveled in displays of mortal combat as did the Romans during the last two centuries B.C. and the first three centuries thereafter, nor derived such pleasure from spectacles in which slaves and convicts were exposed to wild beasts and killed in front of cheering spectators. According to Nicolaus of Damascus, writing in the first decade A.D., Romans even regaled themselves with lethal violence at private banquets; he describes dinner guests relishing the spectacle of gladiators fighting to the death:

> Hosts would invite their friends to dinner not merely for other
> entertainment, but that they might witness two or three pairs
> of contestants in a gladiatorial combat; on these occasions,
> when sated with dining and drink, they called in the gladiators.
> No sooner did one have his throat cut than the masters
> applauded with delight at this feat.[3]

Perhaps the delectation and thrill of viewing a fight to the death at such close hand while reclining after a meal with friends provided even greater pleasure than the vast gladiatorial shows in the amphitheater, in which thousands of combatants confronted death each year. Devotees versed in the aesthetics of violence and the "science of pleasure" could study at close hand the subtleties of the moves in each encounter and celebrate the nobility and beauty with which defeated gladiators who had been denied a reprieve bared their necks for decapitation.[4]

The satiric poet Juvenal's phrase "bread and circuses"—*panem et circenses*—that has come down, through the centuries, to stand for public offerings of nourishment and spectacles on a grand scale, would have meant nothing to the earliest Romans. There is no evidence from their period of vast wild beast hunts in circuses or spectacular forms of capital punishment or gladiatorial combats to the death in the arena. The first gladiatorial fight we know of took place in 264 B.C., when the ex-consul Iunius Brutus Pera and his brother, in a ceremony to honor their dead father, presented three pairs of gladiators in the ox market. More such encounters were offered in the ensuing decades by private citizens as a way to honor dead relatives. But gladiatorial combat was increasingly seen, too, as entertainment and as evidence of generosity, even lavishness on the part of public officials.

Barely two centuries after the first gladiatorial fights, they had become the centerpiece of the Roman "games," alongside wild animal hunts with live game brought from every corner of the known world to be slaughtered, and countless slaves, prisoners, and other victims "thrown to the beasts."[5] Those who died thus were seen either as expendable nonhumans, such as slaves or wild beasts, as criminals or prisoners of war who justly deserved their fate, or as volunteers who had chosen to take part freely or sold themselves into service as gladiators.[6]

Violent spectacles kept the citizenry distracted, engaged, and entertained and, along with reenactments and celebrations of conquests and sacrifices abroad, provided the continued acculturation to violence needed by a warrior state. And the association with bread was constant. Not only were shows in the amphitheater or the circus meant for feasting the eye as well as the emotions: many sponsors also gave out bread, meat, drink, and favorite dishes to the crowds gathered for the games. Elements of entertainment and feasting were combined with ritual and sacrifice. Ancient Rome seems a particularly striking illustration of the claim by literary scholar René Girard that all communal violence can be described in terms of sacrifice, using surrogate victims as means to protect the entire community against its own internal violence.[7] No program could begin without a sacrifice to a deity, often Diana, who presided over the raucous hunting scenes, or Mars, patron of the gladiatorial combats; and after the bloodshed was over, "a figure, representing the powers of the under-world, gave the finishing stroke to the wretches who were still lingering."[8]

Throughout, such violence was regarded as legitimate, fully authorized, even commanded at the highest level of Roman society. The festive atmosphere, the rousing music of the bands, the chanting by the crowds, the betting on who would triumph or lose, the colorful costumes, and the adulation of star gladiators all contributed to the glamour attached to the games. But as historian Kathleen Coleman points out, while "the 'contagion of the throng' may aptly describe the thrill that the Roman spectators experienced in the Colosseum, [it] does not explain why their communal reaction was pleasure instead of revulsion or horror."[9] Part of the reason, she suggests, is that the Roman world "was permeated by violence that had to be absorbed."[10]

Just as Roman spectacles remain the prototype for violent entertainment at its most extreme, so Rome's own history illustrates the development of a prototypical "culture of violence." It was one in which violence was widely sanctioned and hallowed by tradition, in foreign conquest as in domestic culture; in which courage and manhood were exalted and weapons easily available; and in which the climate of brutality and callousness extended from the treatment of newborns and slaves in many homes to the crucifixions and other brutal punishments so common for noncitizens. Entertainment violence officially sponsored on a mass basis served to enhance every one of these aspects of Rome's martial culture.

Among Romans, spectacles of violence had many celebrants and few outspoken challengers. The poet Martial, in his *De Spectaculis*, written in A.D. 80 for the inauguration of the Colosseum, conveyed the magnificence of the fights and wild beast hunts in evocative tones. Speaking of a condemned criminal who, "hanging on no unreal cross gave up his vitals to a Caledonian bear," Martial described his mangled limbs as still living, "though the parts dripped gore, and in all his body was nowhere a body's shape. A punishment deserved at length he won."[11] This death was staged as a performance of the story of Laureolus, a famous bandit leader who had been captured and crucified. This was a favorite subject for dramatic enactment, but as Martial pointed out, the victim in this instance was "hanging on no unreal cross," and his agony was compounded by exposure to the bear.[12]

Why did such spectacles have so few outspoken critics among Romans? We can only wonder at the silence of those, like Marcus Aurelius and Epictetus, who proclaimed Stoic and other ideals of goodness and justice; not to mention the many other philosophers, poets, and legal scholars who were openly admiring of the practice. Like most Romans, they may have been too thoroughly acculturated to violence to see any need for criticism. The historian Tacitus recounts that "there are the peculiar and characteristic vices of this metropolis of ours, taken on, it seems to me, almost in the mother's womb—the passion for play actors and the mania for gladiatorial shows and horse-racing."[13] At home as in the lecture halls, the gossip is all about such spectacles; even the teachers dwell largely on such material in their classes.

Along with such acculturation, fear was the great silencer of outrage and free debate among the Romans and the peoples they conquered. It was dangerous to speak freely, above all to criticize acts of the emperor and practices linked to his worship. At his whim, critics could be jailed, exiled, or thrown to the lions. But more than acculturation and fear was involved. Opportunistic self-censorship was rampant. Many among the intelligentsia and in the aristocracy derived great prestige from sponsoring displays of gladiators. They had a vested interest in seeing the games continue and in deriding criticism.

One who did note a moral paradox in the gladiatorial games presenting violence as public entertainment was the philosopher

Seneca.[14] He pointed to Pompey, reputedly conspicuous among leaders of the state for the kindness of his heart, who had been the first

> to exhibit the slaughter of eighteen elephants in the circus, pitting criminals against them in a mimic battle [and] thought it a notable kind of spectacle to kill human beings after a new fashion. Do they fight to the death? That is not enough! Are they torn to pieces? That is not enough! Let them be crushed by animals of monstrous bulk![15]

That human beings should kill and maim their fellows was hardly paradoxical in its own right; rather, the oddity was that the pleasure in seeing it carried out could be so relished as to override all sense of respect for life: "Man, an object of reverence in the eyes of men, is now slaughtered for jest and sport . . . and it is a satisfying spectacle to see a man made a corpse."[16] For Seneca, sharing the enjoyment of that spectacle brutalized and desensitized viewers and fostered their appetite for still more cruelty. It undercut the central task of seeking to grow in humanity, in nobility of spirit, in understanding, and in freedom from greed, cruelty, and other desires; and thereby to progress toward self-mastery. Seneca saw *any* diversion as deflecting from this task; but taking pleasure in brutality—in "seeing a man made a corpse"—actually reversed the development, destroyed *humanitas*:[17] the respectful kindness that characterizes persons who have learned how to be fully human among humans.[18] Violent entertainments rendered spectators *crudelior et inhumanior*—"more cruel and more inhumane"—acculturating them to pitilessness and to lack of respect for their fellow humans and other creatures.[19]

The same forces that numbed most Romans' shame or sense of moral paradox inherent in relishing such cruelty—acculturation, fear, and profiteering—also helped to dampen criticism in the provinces. Many Roman military encampments had their own amphitheaters, and hundreds of others were built for the public around the Empire in the first centuries A.D. But though Roman authorities and commercial sponsors encouraged attendance at the games in conquered territories as a form of homage to the emperor-deities, such spectacles could not compete in extravagance with those offered by the emperors in Rome and rarely met with the special exultation elsewhere that they evoked there.[20] A few spoke out against them openly: when King Herod wished to offer spectacles in an amphitheater he had constructed near Jerusalem, "the Jews found such a cruel pleasure to be impious and an abandonment of their ancestral customs."[21]

Among the severest critics were Christians, from whose ranks so many were tortured and killed at the games. Late in the second century, Bishop Tertullian thundered, in his *De Spectaculis*, against violent spectacles rooted in pagan religion, with their brutalizing effects on victims, sponsors, combatants, and spectators alike. He lambasted the Christians who took pleasure in such shows and cautioned against the degradation that came, not just from viewing cruelty but from delighting in it, finding it entertaining, developing a "passion for murderous pleasure."[22] With puritanical zeal, he insisted that people should avoid not only violent shows but all spectacles:

> There is no public spectacle without violence to the spirit. For where there is pleasure, there is eagerness, which gives pleasure its flavor. Where there is eagerness, there is rivalry, which gives its flavor to eagerness. Yes, and then, where there is rivalry, there also are madness, bile, anger, pain, and all the things that follow from them and (like them) are incompatible with moral discipline.[23]

Tertullian ended on a shrill note that clashed with all that he had said about the evils of taking pleasure in violent spectacles. He appears to have promised his fellow Christians, in spite of all, the reward of "murderous pleasure" in the next life if they would only abjure it in this one. Reveling in the horrors that would befall those who now took any part in spectacles, he predicted that, come the Day of Judgment, Christians could look forward to the thrill, the exultation at being able to watch, as if they were at the games, the infliction on nonbelievers, such as actors, kings, athletes, poets, and philosophers, of suffering, torture, and burning, horrors far worse than at the earthly games and everlasting to boot:

How vast the spectacle that day, and how wide! What sight shall wake my wonder, what my laughter, my joy, and exultation? As I see all those kings . . . groaning in the depths of darkness! And the magistrates who persecuted the name of Jesus, liquefying in fiercer flames than they kindled in their rage against the Christians! Those sages, too, the philosophers blushing before their disciples as they blaze together . . . and then, the poets trembling before the judgment-seat. . . . And then there will be the tragic actors to be heard, more vocal in their own tragedy; and the players to be seen, lither of limb by far in the fire; . . . Such sights, such exultation—what praetor, consul, quaestor, priest, will ever give you of his bounty? And yet all these, in some sort, are ours, pictured through faith in the imagination of the spirit. But what are those things which eye hath not seen nor ear heard, nor ever entered into the heart of man? I believe, things of greater joy than circus, theatre, amphitheatre, or any stadium.[24]

RECOIL AND
RECOGNITION

After the kill, there is the feast.
And toward the end, when the dancing subsides,
and the young have sneaked off somewhere,
the hounds drunk on the blood of the hares,
begin to talk of how soft
were their pelts, how graceful their leaps,
how lovely their scared, gentle eyes.

LISEL MUELLER,
"SMALL POEM ABOUT THE HOUNDS AND THE HARES"[25]

Revulsion against the Roman gladiatorial games intensified during the third century. By the fourth, they had become for many what one historian calls "an unthinkable monstrosity."[26] But even though they were outlawed again and again, they would flare up each time, until they were finally abolished for good in 438. Ever since, historians of the period have spoken of the chasm that separates us from the Romans in this regard. Keith Hopkins refers to the games, with their "welter of blood in gladiatorial and wild-beast shows, the squeals of the victims and of slaughtered animals," as "completely alien to us and almost unimaginable"; and Samuel Dill stresses our difficulty in conceiving of the fascination that the spectacles in the amphitheater and the theater had, "not only on characters hardened by voluptuousness, but on the cultivated and humane."[27]

Just how unimaginable are the Roman practices to today's publics? Most people would recoil from the thought of banquets such as those described at the beginning of this chapter, offering guests the chance to feast not only on food and drink but also on gladiatorial combat. Even so, they might recognize the emotions underlying the guests' delight in viewing such fights at close hand and their aesthetic appreciation of the combatants' skill.

As we strive to understand in what sense the Roman practices might nevertheless be "completely alien" to us, we have to ask whether our contemporary versions of entertainment violence exhibit anything like the paradox inherent in the role of the gladiatorial games as public entertainment. This is not to say that our societies are at any risk of tolerating public spectacles such as Rome's. Our laws prohibit them, and our institutions allow the open debate and criticism that Romans could not have. Rather, what matters for us is to explore the uncomfortable present-day parallels to the thrill and joyful entertainment associated with watching bloodshed, the function of the games in acculturating the Romans to violence, and the exploiting of even the bloodthirstiest practices by Rome's commercial and political vested interests, not to mention the self-censorship practiced by many of its authors, artists, and critics.

Consider present-day bullfights, cockfights, or bouts of "ultimate" or "extreme" fighting, in which two combatants "do whatever they can—absent biting and eye-gouging—to send each other into unconsciousness or submission. They kick, they probe, they grapple, often on mats that quickly become slick with sweat and blood."[28] Outlawed in some states, permitted in others, such games draw large crowds and hundreds of thousands of TV spectators. Would not at least some among them likewise thrill to watch human combatants fight to the death?

To Sigmund Freud, there would be nothing alien about contemporaries delighting in such spectacles. In discussing the aggressiveness that he took to be an instinctual characteristic of human beings, Freud quoted the words of the Roman playwright Plautus, *"Homo homini lupus"*—"Man is a wolf to man." Freud viewed aggressiveness among humans is one expression of *Thanatos*, the drive toward death and destruction that is opposed and harnessed to the drive toward life, creativity, and love, or *Eros*:

> Their neighbour is for them not only a potential helper or
> sexual object, but also someone who tempts them to satisfy
> their aggressiveness on him, to exploit his capacity for work
> without compensation, to use him sexually without his
> consent, to seize his possessions, to humiliate him, to cause
> him pain, to torture and to kill him.[29]

Few still speak of such instincts today; and on the basis of the research done since Freud's time on the development both of aggression and of empathy, more are now prepared to view them as acquired through imitation and practice, even as they are based on inborn predispositions. Thus the biologist Edward O. Wilson suggests that aggressive behavior is learned, but that the learning is prepared in that "we are strongly predisposed to slide into deep, irrational hostility under certain definable conditions. With dangerous ease hostility feeds on itself and ignites runaway reactions that can swiftly progress to alienation and violence."[30] For Wilson, as for Freud, Simone Weil, and others who have studied aggression, the arts are central to the prospects for civilization to counter and constrain and deflect the human potential for destruction.[31] Music, literature, theater, and spectacles of every kind enhance the chances for human thriving, even as they have also been enlisted, most strikingly in Rome as in our own century's totalitarian states, for purposes of aggression.

Both sorts of potential have been vastly enhanced by modern technology. Our worldwide distribution systems, piping programs into hundreds of millions of homes at all hours, go beyond anything the Romans, adept as they were at engineering feats, could have imagined. By now, the American entertainment industry produces and trades in violent programming on an ever vaster scale; and it aims its products with increasing precision at children and adolescents.[32] Not that children were excluded from crowds watching boxing matches or bullfights or even the bloodiest slaughter in the Roman arenas. But never before have children been targeted as a lucrative market for entertainment violence and for toys, games, and paraphernalia associated with particular programs; nor have marketing experts studied with such care the factors heightening the "audience arousal" that draws television viewers in and facilitates their acceptance of advertising messages. In previous generations, children had little money to spend; they now influence the flow of vast sums: in 1997, it was estimated that American children 14 and under would directly spend $20 billion and would influence the spending of another $200 billion.[33]

As the profitability and the amount of violent entertainment grow, as technology is improved for presenting it more graphically and realistically, and as children are increasingly seen as targeted and at risk, public concerns deepen. However forceful the disagreements about the extent to which the allure of violence is inherent in the human species or, on the contrary, culturally fostered, it is clear that children are made, not born, to be consumers of entertainment violence on today's scale.

Polls show that Americans are deeply ambivalent about how to respond. Even many adults who acknowledge the thrill they derive from films such as *Natural Born Killers* and *Silence of the Lambs* worry about the hypnotic power the screen exercises over children and young people. Among adult respondents to one 1995 poll, 21 percent blamed television more than *any* other factor for teenage sex and violence.[34] But public concern goes beyond the question of whether consumers of entertainment violence turn out, in the long run, to be more aggressive in real life, to focus on the desensitization and the arousal of greater and greater appetite for the thrill that entertainment violence can bring. Yet even as parents worry about the messages on television about drugs, sex, and brutality, they rely on it for keeping children busy, and most set no limits whatsoever on the amount of television their children see.[35] Indeed, Americans of all ages go to great lengths and expense to seek out the very forms of entertainment that so many condemn in polls. They flock to blockbuster movies that "push the envelope" with respect to graphic brutality and take in countless TV shows featuring domestic violence, rape, child abuse, gang violence, and serial killers.

THE THRILL OF
THE KILL

*What constitutes the painful voluptuousness of tragedy is
cruelty; what seems agreeable in so-called tragic pity, and at
bottom in everything sublime, up to the highest and most
delicate shudders of metaphysics, receives its sweetness solely
from the admixture of cruelty. What the Roman in the arena,
the Christian in the ecstasies of the cross, the Spaniard at an
auto-da-fe or bullfight, . . .—what all of them enjoy and seek
to drink in with mysterious ardor are the spicy potions of the
great Circe, "cruelty."*

FRIEDRICH NIETZSCHE, *BEYOND GOOD AND EVIL*[36]

Nietzsche, who celebrated the Romans as the strongest, noblest people who ever lived and every vestige of them "a sheer delight," has no
rival among philosophers in extolling cruelty as central, liberating, and
exhilarating in human culture.[37] Yet few might disagree with him
about the pleasure such cruelty can give to devotees of blood sport,
whether in ancient Rome or today. He links the thrill of witnessing
violence both to consuming and to the erotic. Both aspects are at issue
in his references to the ardor with which people drink in cruelty during
spectacles of violence.[38] Discussing murder stories, literary scholar

Wendy Lesser likewise holds that they "stimulate the hunger they purport to feed, offering us a few morsels but leaving us, finally, with our own unappeasable ravenousness"—an urge that she sees as underlying also the taste for violent films and for watching "live" or televised public executions. [39]

But even as people in all periods have derived sensual, aesthetic, at times erotic thrills from witnessing fights to the death or public hangings, it would be wrong to conclude that spectators at such events and consumers of media violence are guided by no other motives. Romans went to the arenas as many go to boxing matches today, in part to while away the time, to eat and drink and gossip and cheer for their favorite combatants.

Vicarious terror can also be pleasurable, as spectators test their reactions to mortal danger without having to run the actual risks. Seeing humans and animals fight, sometimes for their lives, allows viewers to engage indirectly in their travails and to test their own responses to terror—to confront the reality of horror and cruelty from which they ordinarily shield themselves. Wes Craven, director of such horror films as *A Nightmare on Elm Street* and *Scream*, suggests that "in scary movies, we are looking behind the scrim of propriety and finding things not pretty to look at, ancient in nature and primal in their importance."[40] For Craven as for Nietzsche, such works challenge our instinctive denial of our most primitive layers of fear and aggression. By entering into the excitement and the power of inflicting pain or death and the terror of seeing these up close, they suggest, we may also learn to steel ourselves, to become better able to "take" the violence before our eyes. A common accompaniment of such learning is to come to look at the infliction of suffering in a purely aesthetic way: to make judgments about the expertise or the strength or the courage of the combatants, or to look for elements of beauty in the encounter itself.

The confrontation with one's own fears and the vicarious sharing of risks to life and limb are also among the attractions of disaster stories and movies, as of news accounts of floods, earthquakes, and hurricanes. In these "spectacles," however, because there is little or no intended cruelty behind the horrors that befall victims, the paradoxical pleasure found in the carnage that humans inflict on one another is absent. Here, the terror of the circumstances often blends with pity for the victims—something entirely different from the pitilessness that accompanies much entertainment violence.

What about war movies, detective stories, and cops-and-robbers accounts, in which viewers are presented with confrontations between right and wrong, good and evil? The killing of villains occurs as a dramatic device or a form of closure rather than something to be savored for its cruelty. It is often the "element of precipitousness" in such confrontations that attracts us most forcefully, as William James points out:

> What excites and interests the looker-on at life, what the
> romances and the statues celebrate and the grim civic
> monuments remind us of, is the everlasting battle of the
> powers of light with those of darkness; with heroism reduced
> to its barest chance, yet ever and anon snatching victory from
> the jaws of death.[41]

Many accounts of such battles involve no more exultation in cruelty than do disaster movies. A Sherlock Holmes or Agatha Christie plot differs utterly, in this regard, from a mystery in which viewers are invited to sympathize with the killer. So do action films like *Independence Day*, that appeal to the sense of delight we know from childhood in wreaking havoc, knocking down towers, and seeing fireworks explode and buildings crumble to dust. It is when the harm done to the victims is to be enjoyed for its own sake that the paradox of entertainment violence is most striking to the uninitiated.

Whatever extra elements may draw spectators to violent entertainment of this kind, it is the thrill derived from the violence itself that is often highlighted in movie and video game advertisements. For example, publicity for Kathryn Bigelow's film *Strange Days*, that offers viewers the vicarious experience of rape and killing, touts the film as "a troubling but undeniably breathless joy ride," a "wild, mind-blowing spectacle," and a "combination of adrenaline rush and cold sweat"; and players of the video game Carmageddon are invited to "waste counterparts, pedestrians, and farmyard animals for points and credits!"[42]

It is this intense pleasure in watching violence done in which Nietzsche exulted and which Seneca condemned in speaking of the "satisfying spectacle to see a man made a corpse." The experience of that pleasure has rarely been more vividly described than by Saint Augustine in an incident involving lovers of gladiatorial games, recounted in his *Confessions.* In 380 he was a young teacher of rhetoric already renowned for his brilliance, not yet a convert to Christianity but outspoken against the frenzy of spectacles and distressed to see his young friend Alypius addicted to them. Augustine succeeded in convincing Alypius to give up this passion; but later, in Rome, Alypius fell for the blandishments of friends begging him to go along with them to see gladiators fight in the amphitheater. Even as he went with them, he protested that at least they would not be able to force him to look at what went on with open eyes:

> When they arrived at the arena, the place was seething with the lust for cruelty. They found seats as best they could and Alypius shut his eyes tightly, determined to have nothing to do with these atrocities. If only he could have closed his ears as well! For an incident in the fight drew a great roar from the crowd, and this thrilled him so deeply that he could not contain his curiosity. . . . So he opened his eyes, and his soul was stabbed with a wound more deadly than any which the gladiator, whom he was so anxious to see, had received in his body. He fell, and fell more pitifully than the man whose fall had drawn the roar of excitement from the crowd. The din had pierced his ears and forced him to open his eyes, laying his soul open to receive the wound which struck it down. . . .
>
> When he saw the blood, it was as though he had drunk a deep draught of savage passion. Instead of turning away, he fixed his eyes upon the scene and drank in all its frenzy, unaware of what he was doing. He reveled in the wickedness

of the fighting and was drunk with the fascination of bloodshed. . . . He watched and cheered and grew hot with excitement, and when he left the arena, he carried away with him a diseased mind which would leave him no peace until he came back again, no longer simply with the friends who had first dragged him there, but at their head, leading new sheep to the slaughter.[43]

This passage has resonated throughout subsequent debates about violent entertainment.[44] Augustine conveyed both his perception of the craving for still more bloodshed that the thrill of the games could arouse and his conviction that such experiences threaten grave harm to spectators—harm for which he used the metaphor the "stabbing of the soul."

Some have thought his portrayal overwrought; others have taken it to be as true of violent entertainment in our time as in Augustine's. For the purpose of our contemporary discussions, his example raises two questions. They concern the nature of the harm imputed to spectators themselves—to their souls, as he put it—and the risks that spectators thus debilitated might pose to others. Are they rendered more uncaring about suffering as a result of having partaken of carnage as entertainment, more pitiless, perhaps even more easily moved to aggression?

How seriously must we take Augustine's conviction about damage to the spectators in considering our own entertainment violence? Clearly, there is hyperbole in his calling the wound to Alypius's soul more deadly than any that the fallen gladiator had received in his body. Augustine was not a teacher of rhetoric for nothing. In fact, his young friend went on to renounce the games, convert to Christianity, and become a bishop. What is meant, in that case, by the "stabbing of the soul"? Did Augustine imply that there is a link between the thrill in witnessing murder and mayhem and the excitement that can accompany actually *engaging* in such acts in real life?

Among all those who relish the brutality of corpse-strewn slasher films, only a small fraction are capable of perpetrating lethal violence themselves. Even among the latter, only a minority experience an intense thrill in the process, as opposed to emotional numbness, shame, or rage. Criminologist James Alan Fox distinguishes the "thrill" killer from the "mission" killer and the "expedient" killer: only those in the first category, he suggests, derive pleasure from the sheer act of killing.[45] Some of these fortify themselves with films and fantasies of sadistic acts in order to "live them out," as Joyce Carol Oates points out in her review of books on the subject, "I Had No Other Thrill or Happiness."[46] Citing serial killer Ted Bundy's claim "I'm in charge of entertainment," Oates characterizes such killers as "individuals whose self-definition, whose sole *happiness* is bound up with killing."[47] A large public, in turn, finds their exploits mesmerizing. Oates suggests that their highly publicized crimes, along with often sentimentalizing books, films, and poetry about them, have contributed to serial killing being "the crime of the nineties."

No matter how intrigued people may be by accounts and images of such carnage, the average man or woman feels intense instinctive resistance to actually killing a fellow human, even in self-defense or what they take to be a just war. But it is also the case that many, especially the young, can be conditioned to overcome such resistance by means of well-known training techniques.[48] They can be more easily persuaded that it is right to engage in killing when such action is held out as legitimate, authorized, commanded; still more when it is portrayed as glamorous, admirable, heroic, and deserving of imitation and when the victims are held to be unworthy of ordinary concern and respect, perhaps less than human or as having chosen to take the risk of dying. Together these influences, when successful, generate a heightened sense of rightness about the act of killing, drawing on its felt necessity and glamour as well as on a lack of pity for the putative victims.

Depending on the suggestibility of those exposed, these influences can serve not only to support legitimate individual and collective self-defense but also to facilitate every form of aggression. At such times, they can weaken the most basic respect for humanity and in turn, at least for short periods, anesthetize the shame, inculcated since childhood, of violating that respect. It is at this point that the "combat high," the "thrill of the kill" described by combat veterans can take over[49]—a feeling that resonates in the words attributed to twelfth-century Mongol ruler Genghis Khan, that life's greatest joy is to "kill your enemies, make their beloved weep, ride on their horses, embrace their wives and daughters."

Those who have crossed even the most basic moral boundaries in such a fashion have made themselves nearly impervious to criticism. It is of no avail, William James held, to attempt to dissuade those who have come to love war by pointing to its horror: "The horror makes the thrill."[50] What is often left out of larger debates about war and all other violence, he suggests, is precisely that core of sheer thrill. For James, engaging in violence is one of the paths (along with intoxication by alcohol and other substances) to what he calls a "radiant core" of consciousness that can focus, illuminate, and intensify experience—a core that can give the sense, momentarily, of opposites welded together, of single-mindedness in the midst of chaos, of all fear and shame and awareness of transgression temporarily erased. But these shortcuts to mystical experience and to brief visions of vitality, insight, and oneness with truth give but momentary access to what James calls the "steeps of life."[51]

Even if we see a link between the thrill some people derive from engaging in actual combat and from being a spectator to such combat, however, there are clearly immense differences between the two. How then can we tell whether the three influences mentioned above—authorization, glamorization, and induced pitilessness—accustom and enable spectators to experience heightened pleasure from violence? And why should we care, if no actual violence to third parties is at issue?

Some critics of media violence are convinced that these influences do affect viewers, beginning in childhood. They point out that most families provide authorization to enjoy entertainment violence and that the story lines themselves in violent shows—involving, for example, cops and robbers or warfare or attacks by aliens—offer further legitimacy; that screen violence is often rendered more glamorous than real-life combat; and that pitilessness is greatly encouraged by seeing scenes of torture and murder recur innumerable times on the screen and being able to record and replay them at will in ways not remotely possible in real life even for the most obsessive killer. What these critics still have to ask, however, is whether becoming inured to entertainment violence in such ways is harmful to the persons so affected and whether there is any carryover effect into real life that can place others at risk.

One commentator, Colonel Dave Grossman, suggests that the same techniques that military trainers use to prepare recruits to kill are now provided in the media.[52] Because even the youngest children experience influences such as habituation to violence and desensitization, their effects are much more indiscriminate, without the distinctions made in the military between targets that are legitimate and those that are not. Children are exposed to these influences long before they understand the distinction between fact and fiction, between right and wrong, between shame and shamelessness—and as a result, long before they have the tools for giving their free and informed consent to the conditioning that they are unwittingly undergoing.

Others disagree vehemently with any implication that the depiction of violence need have deleterious effects on viewers, much less on third parties. Some go further, to underscore its benefits. According to media analyst Lawrence Jarvik, such depiction "reflects a fundamental confidence in individual freedom and personal liberty. Repeated illustrations of violence and immorality are necessary to impart ethical lessons to the citizenry just as 'hellfire and brimstone' are used in sermons to emphasize the frightening prospect of hell."[53] For most people, the strongest reason for skepticism about whether entertainment violence brings about anything like Augustine's "stabbing of the soul" is that they are not viewing actual bloodshed in a crowd but sitting at home in front of their screens watching cartoons and movies. Their participation is of an entirely different nature; the violence and suffering they witness are staged; and the persons involved are actors or animated characters. Why draw comparisons, in that case, between most entertainment violence and the carnage in the arenas, or suggest that cartoons and movies damage spectators?

''BUT MOVIES ARE NOT REAL''

I mean it's a western, it's entertaining, it's good guys versus bad guys. In that scene in "The Searchers" when John Wayne went after all those Indians, was that genocide? Was that racist? When James Bond dropped the guy in a pond of piranhas, and he says "Bon appétit," we loved that. That's a great moment. Movies are not real. JOEL SILVER[54]

Why should moviegoers *not* love James Bond's quip as he drops his adversary into the piranha pond in *You Only Live Twice*? Or hesitate to relish the explosions and up-close shootings in blockbuster films such as producer Joel Silver's *Die Hard* and the *Lethal Weapon* series? Granted, such actions qualify as violent by any definition. But consumers of entertainment violence who enjoy them are, after all, neither doing any harm in their own right nor witnessing real-life carnage and mayhem. Where is the harm, if no real violence is done?

The vicarious participation of movie publics is of an entirely different nature from that of Romans in the arena. As director John Woo—variously dubbed "the poet of spilled blood" and "the Mozart of mayhem"—puts it, "Violence in real life is horrid, frightening. Movies are fake, not real. People know that movies are not real."[55] The

35

difference between what is and is not real in films must be especially glaring to anyone involved, as are Silver and Woo, in the actual production of movies. To them, what is real is precisely not the artifacts they produce. It is, rather, their work with the actors, the stage sets, the makeup personnel, the costuming, the cameras, and all that goes into creating the appearance of reality for viewers.

At times, however, the two worlds come close, even for Holly-wood professionals. When Joel Silver protested that movies are not real, he was responding to those who criticized his timing in opening his film *Lethal Weapon 3* in May 1992. Only weeks earlier the Los Angeles police officers whose roadside beating of motorist Rodney King had been shown on TV screens the world over had been acquitted by an all-white jury. The verdict had sparked outbreaks of looting, burning, and killing that left thirty-seven persons dead and more than fifteen hundred injured, even as fires burned out of control for days. In that crisis, the boundaries between movies and reality blurred, not only for the public but also for Hollywood producers, directors, and actors who were seeing smoke rising beneath their hillside residences and hearing sirens echo up and down the canyons. The newsreel footage of store owners terrorized, of victims trampled underfoot, of families watching their homes burning out of control was suddenly all too similar to the most brutal of the films from which Silver and his colleagues made their living. Of course they would have known how to stage the mayhem and pyrotechnics to still greater effect for viewers, using state-of-the-art special effects. But the differences between the two worlds, just then, were no longer quite so self-evident.

Producers, directors, actors, and others in the entertainment industry are increasingly rethinking the initial response of simply rejecting any responsibility for societal ills through claims about their products not being real. When polled, many are troubled by the impact of media violence.[56] It is clear to growing numbers among them, as among the public, that while the distinction between what is real and what is enacted or reenacted is indispensable, it cannot suffice to terminate discussions of the effects of media violence. Although the violence in movies and TV programs is often fictional or at least reenacted and thus is not actually carried out on real victims, movies as such are surely real in most other senses of the term. A killing in a movie is watched by real people on whom it may have real effects. (In news programs, documentaries, and many "infotainment" programs, moreover, the violence itself is "real" in Silver's sense as well; and in fringe underground so-called "snuff films," murder is expressly carried out and filmed live to cater to the tastes of viewers.)

The screen renders experience both less and more real in its own right. It both mediates violence and makes it seem more immediate, exposing viewers to levels and forms of violence they might never otherwise encounter. It helps cross boundaries between real and reenacted, between art and entertainment, between being near the violence and being at a distance. In "virtual reality" offerings of experiences of gunplay and combat, the whole point is to erase the boundary between what is and is not experienced as real. Video technology offers the possibility of revisiting violent scenes at will, even as it permits viewers to click off and tune out. At times the only lack of reality in films for viewers comes from the fact that they have no personal responsibility for inflicting or enjoying whatever brutality they are witnessing. They can cross even that boundary vicariously in participatory computer games such as Mortal Kombat in which players are rewarded for slashing, gouging, or shooting their opponents. In recent years, video games have become increasingly graphic in presenting elaborate death sequences in highly realistic detail. "First person shooter" games such as Doom, Quake, and Duke Nukem enable players to see with the eyes of the killer holding the gun.

Questions about degrees of reality and about the role of real-life, imagined, and reenacted violence in our lives are crucial to our learning to understand and to deal with violence. But these questions cannot be dismissed, much less resolved, by making tidy distinctions between the real and the not-real. Nor should the public debate about entertainment violence be prematurely dismissed on such grounds. There are no watertight barriers between the real and the not-real, least of all when it comes to the imagination. The same holds true for the chasms some would conjure up between entertainment and art, education, or news—none of which suffices to isolate or explain or demystify entertainment violence, least of all to tame it, to strip it of the potential for providing the deep inward thrill that *doing* violence can also bring.

The boundaries between reality and unreality are especially permeable for small children. They are unable, through at least the age of three or four, to distinguish fact from fantasy. Even older children rarely manage to keep "real life" and vicarious experience in watertight compartments.[57] Children are also more likely to conclude that violence on the screen reflects real-life abuses if they have personal experience of abuse in their family or neighborhood. For them, what they witness at home and on the streets reinforces what they see enacted on the screen. They are exposed, before they are in any position to distinguish what they see on the screen from real life, to amounts and levels of entertainment violence that are potentially more brutalizing than many adults—parents, script writers, and TV producers among them—realize.

In Britain, the video *Child's Play* 3 was at issue when two ten-year-olds tormented, then murdered a toddler, James Bulger, after viewing it; and later when a teenager, Suzanne Capper, was kidnapped, tortured, and set alight by a group of young acquaintances who chanted the catchphrase from the video: "I'm Chucky. Wanna play?" The novelist Martin Amis points out that the video has in turn

> been set alight, semi-ritualistically by public-spirited managers of video-rental stores. When my two children (aged seven and nine) noticed *Child's Play* 3 in its package, up on a high shelf, they regarded it with reverent dread. In their schoolyard voodoo, *Child's Play* 3 was considered potent, venomous, toxic. It was like angel dust—a ticket to frenzy.[58]

Amis concludes that Chucky is unlikely to affect anything but the *style* of atrocities. "Murderers have to have something to haunt them; they need their internal pandemonium. A century ago, it might have been the Devil. Now it's Chucky."[59] But about the ten-year-old throwing bricks at James Bulger, Amis concludes on a note of greater doubt concerning, precisely, the distinction between reality and make-believe: "Perhaps, also, the child did not understand the meaning of earnest. As a result, he was all too ready to play."[60]

TRANSFORMING VIOLENCE

"However, we haven't yet made the greatest accusation against imitation. [mimesis] For the fact that it succeeds in maiming even the decent men, except for a certain rare few, is surely quite terrible. . . . Whenever the best of us hear Homer or any other of the tragic poets imitating one of the heroes in mourning and making quite an extended speech with lamentation, or, if you like, singing and beating his breast, you know that we enjoy it and that we give ourselves over to following the imitation; suffering along with the hero in all seriousness, we praise as a good poet the man who most puts us in this state. . . . But when personal sorrow comes to one of us, you are aware that, on the contrary, we pride ourselves if we are able to able to keep quiet and bear up, taking this to be the part of a man and what we then praised to be that of a woman. . . . Is that a fine way to praise?" I said. "We see a man whom we would not condescend, but would rather blush, to resemble, and, instead of being disgusted, we enjoy and praise it?"

PLATO, *THE REPUBLIC,* BOOK X[61]

Plato had no doubts about the power of poetry and all imitation in art to have what he called a "maiming" effect on listeners and viewers. There could be no place even for the greatest poets in his ideal city.

Disagreements concerning the effects of violence conveyed in works of art and entertainment have resonated, over the centuries, with the terms he and Aristotle employed concerning imitation in art more generally.[62] Iris Murdoch suggests, in *The Fire and the Sun: Why Plato Banished the Artists*, that because Plato viewed human life as a pilgrimage from appearance to reality, and held that works of art constituted imitation capable of impeding this quest, they had to be strictly censored not least when they depict evil and cruelty. When artists imitate what is bad, they are adding to the sum of badness in the world, so that "images of wickedness and excess may lead even good people to indulge secretly through art feelings which they would be ashamed to entertain in real life. We enjoy cruel jokes and bad taste in the theatre, then behave boorishly at home."[63]

The challenge to such a view has relied on one or both of two arguments about art's transforming power: that it can transform either the subject matter it represents or its recipients in ways that nullify maiming or other damaging effects, and at times also bring about purification and ennoblement. Picturing or describing a violent scene, first of all, can shed light on it in such a way that it provides, at the very least, harmless amusement, possibly insight and joy. As both Plato and Aristotle pointed out, we do delight in representations of objects and emotions that would evoke altogether different responses in real life; but most of us side with Aristotle in refusing to regard this as corrupting or maiming in its own right. We laugh at the pratfalls and pies thrown at people's faces in slapstick movies as we would not in real life. We relish works of art such as the Vatican's *Laocoön* or Picasso's *Guernica*. The seventeenth-century French poet and art critic Nicolas Boileau went so far as to say that there is no monster or odious serpent that does not please the eye when imitated by art; the agreeable artifice of a delicate paintbrush can make "a lovable object" out of the most horrific one.[64]

If all depiction of monsters and of acts of cruelty and evils more generally could transform them thus into "lovable objects," there might be no paradox in today's concept of entertainment violence. But it is hard to see how Boileau's statement can be extended in this way. He was speaking of classical tragedy and painting, both of which offer an aesthetic distance that is absent from much of contemporary violent entertainment. And he specified, as had Aristotle and Horace, that some horrors are better merely recounted, as in classical tragedy, than conveyed visually: too much resemblance to reality would generate the same recoil at the sight of what was depicted as that aroused by the real object.[65] It is precisely the massive visual presence on home screens of either realistic or stylized violence for entertainment purposes that both worries and attracts many in the public today. Even as we accept the first challenge to Plato's condemnation of imitation in art on Aristotelian grounds, therefore, this conclusion does not remove the need to examine the effects of such media violence.

Could the second challenge to Plato's views be of greater relevance in this regard? It holds that portrayals of violence can transform the viewers themselves, not simply their perception of the violence depicted; and that this transformation can act upon viewers in such a way as to cleanse their emotions. According to director Martin Verhoefen, it is "a kind of purifying experience to watch violence."[66] Perhaps such works can transform and purify viewers by granting them insight into violence without their having to experience it or be tempted to engage in it in their own lives. In that case, the programs in question would not only represent mere harmless entertainment but would also make possible great moral benefits for viewers.

The notion of art as purging viewers has come down over the centuries, entering common parlance as an echo of Aristotle's complex working out of the concept of *catharsis*. Aristotle insists, as against Plato, that there need be nothing wrong with imitation. It is natural for us to engage in imitative play and activities from childhood on. We know from experience that "though the objects themselves may be painful to see, we delight to view the most realistic representations of them in art, the forms, for example, of the lowest animals and of dead bodies."[67] Tragic drama and epics such as the *Iliad* can so treat the course of human lives as to allow those who listen to "thrill with horror and melt to pity at what takes place," to bring about a "proper purgation of these emotions."[68]

> A tragedy, then, is the imitation of an action that is serious and also, as having magnitude, complete in itself; in language with pleasurable accessories, each kind brought in separately in the parts of the work; in a dramatic, not in a narrative form; with incidents arousing pity and fear, wherewith to accomplish its catharsis of such emotions.[69]

This experience of *catharsis* permits a schooling of the emotions and a deepening of one's understanding of human nature and of the paradoxes relating to the role of violence in human life. It can bring what the literary scholar Walter Jackson Bate has called "an enlargement of the soul by sympathetic identification with the tragic character and the tragic situation."[70]

Those who stretch the concept of *catharsis* so as to claim that it occurs in viewing violence more generally have to address the issue of the schooling of the emotions and the enlargement of the soul that it makes possible. Without such sympathetic identification brought about by the experience of both fear and pity, there can be no *catharsis* in the Aristotelian sense. For Aristotle, Homer's *Iliad* and *Odyssey* and the tragedies of Sophocles—the very works that Plato wished to banish—could allow *catharsis*, but only for adults mature enough to derive the fullest benefit from such an experience. Part of the schooling of the emotions to which such works can contribute, moreover, involves gaining fuller insight into the role of violence in human lives that we ordinarily do so much to avoid confronting.

Such *catharsis*, however, is precisely not at issue in much entertainment violence. Whether or not taking delight in spectacles of bloodshed inflicts a "stabbing of the soul," few would claim that it automatically produces an "enlargement of the soul." At the same time, however, there clearly are films and television programs and works of art that arouse both fear and pity in ways that can have transformative effects on viewers—as much in our day as in past periods. It matters as urgently now as then to consider what it is about works such as Picasso's *Guernica* and Steven Spielberg's film *Schindler's List* that sets them apart from productions of entertainment violence.

Some envisage *catharsis* in the contemporary therapeutic sense of "abreaction," the release of anxiety through reliving episodes in one's past, or of acting out aggression, contempt, or hatred in imagination. Sigmund Freud developed the "cathartic method" as a therapy whereby patients could unburden their minds by "bringing the sub-merged painful experience to consciousness, thus releasing the strangulated emotions."[71] Perhaps there is some echo of this Freudian sense of the word in director Martin Scorsese's remark about our needing "the *catharsis* of blood-letting and decapitation like the Ancient Romans needed it." But *catharsis* in the classical sense could hardly be at issue in Roman gladiatorial games, since they were not dramatic imitations (*mimesis*) but the real thing. Whatever terror the carnage in the arenas produced, its accompaniment was predominantly thrill rather than pity.[72] As Pliny said, it inspired citizens to "a glory in wounds and a contempt of death, since the love of praise and desire for victory could be seen, even in the bodies of slaves and criminals."[73]

The Freudian view of *catharsis* as a working through or "abreaction" of painful personal experiences involves, as does Aristotle's, learning to feel and perceive more fully, and to reflect more deeply on the role of violence. Simplified versions of both views lend themselves to a third, still more recent interpretation of the word as "letting off steam," allowing individuals to vent dammed-up energies that could otherwise find dangerous outlets in real life.[74] *Catharsis* in this sense has received considerable attention from social scientists studying the effects of television violence on children.[75] If violent films, videos, television shows, and interactive games could be shown to have such an effect, this would constitute a benefit to be weighed against other, more debilitating effects.

In the early years of television, when far less graphic violence was available on the screen, a few studies claimed to show such a "catharsis effect." Investigators held that at least some adolescents who saw violence on the screen were able to release pent-up emotion and exhibit less aggression as a result.[76] Such claims are occasionally still made: thus media studies professor Jib Fowles holds that by having "television entertainment with adequate sex and violence, Americans are nightly able to empty their subconscious; aggressive fantasies produce tranquil minds."[77] By now, however, most media scholars regard this "catharsis theory" as having been disproved for children and adolescents, as well as for those adults who admit that violent programs stimulate aggressive thoughts, sometimes actions.[78]

The concept of *catharsis* is crucial to our understanding of when works of art contribute to an enlargement or a stabbing of the soul. But when this concept is bloated to encompass the effects of all entertainment violence, whether among the Romans or in today's media culture, it becomes useless for making such distinctions.

The stakes are high. Because of the scope that entertainment violence has assumed, the new technological and marketing means at the disposal of its producers, and the importance of considering any linkage it may have to societal violence, we have greater reason than ever to inquire into its effects. Does present-day programming constitute "harmless entertainment"? Has it become something of a scapegoat in societies unwilling or unable to undertake serious measures to curb crime? To what extent can it help legitimate violence, glamorize it, perhaps desensitize viewers and arouse the need for more frequent and more intensive exposure?

PART TWO
the impact of media violence

There can no longer be any doubt that heavy exposure to televised violence is one of the causes of aggressive behavior, crime, and violence in society. The evidence comes from both the laboratory and real-life studies. Television violence affects youngsters of all ages, of both genders, at all socio-economic levels and all levels of intelligence. The effect is not limited to children who are already disposed to being aggressive and is not restricted to this country. The fact that we get this same finding of a relation between television violence and aggression in children in study after study, in one country after another, cannot be ignored. The causal effect of television violence on aggression, even though it is not very large, exists. . . . We have come to believe that a vicious cycle exists in which television violence makes children more aggressive and these aggressive children turn to watching more and more violence to justify their own behavior.

LEONARD ERON,
"THE IMPACT OF TELEVISION VIOLENCE," 1992[1]

Gory programs usher children into an otherwise forbidden world, where they can vicariously vent their frustrations and hostilities. Seething resentments and impulses toward unspeakable cruelties can be spent in a way that is not absolutely chastised by society, one that is—more important, from the small child's point of view— totally free of any chance for hurtful retaliation. . . . Striving in school, earning a living, or maintaining a household brings pleasures and benefits, to be sure, but there are more than a few costs. It is televised fantasies that help make up for those costs. Whenever television is blamed for our failings, a criminal disservice and misunderstanding is being perpetuated; the cure is being treated as the curse.

JIB FOWLES,
*WHY VIEWERS WATCH:
A REAPPRAISAL OF TELEVISION'S EFFECTS,* 1992[2]

DOUBLE TAKES

Imagine that Rip van Winkle had slept almost two centuries instead of twenty years, only to wake up in 1995 in the town of Hudson, New York, while *Frontline* reporter Al Austin and his associates were filming the documentary "Does TV Kill?" In Washington Irving's story, the indolent, henpecked Rip had been used to rambling about the little town where he lived and hearing children shout with joy when he approached, "knowing how he assisted at their sports, made their play things, taught them to fly kites and shoot marbles, and told them long stories of ghosts, witches and Indians," only to wake up twenty years older and find that

> Strange names were over the doors—strange faces at the windows—every thing was strange. His mind now misgave him; he began to doubt whether both he and the world around him were bewitched.[3]

This time, Rip would discover an entirely new town where his village had been. He would see fewer children at play outdoors. Instead, he would find them sitting indoors, often in front of television sets, some of them in turn being observed and filmed by Austin and his television crew, who had come to Hudson with psychologist Leonard Eron, for the purpose of "watching people watching television":

> This is where the Headless Horseman rode and Rip van Winkle slept. Columbia County, in the Catskills; Hudson, New York. An old town with deep wrinkles. Uncomfortable with the changes it sees all around. . . . *Frontline* came to Hudson because this is where television was born. And it was among the people here, more than anywhere else in the world, that experts have worked to learn what television does to us; and here that they first found a connection between television and violence.[4]

Austin and Eron had received permission from several families to train cameras both on the children and others watching television and on the sets themselves, in order to study how viewing habits, home conditions, and child-rearing practices might relate to aggressive behavior in children.

When Eron had first interviewed 835 third graders in Columbia County in 1960, he had been surprised by the role he found television played in their lives. The more violent the programs they watched at home, the more aggressive they were in school. He came back in 1971, and again in 1980, to reinterview the same subjects and found that a higher proportion of those who had been heavy consumers of TV violence as children also turned out to have problems with violence in late adolescence and early adulthood. The more aggressive they had been at eight, moreover, the more aggressive they tended to be at thirty: they logged more arrests and more criminal convictions, were more aggressive in their homes, and had more aggressive children.[5] Now, in 1993, Eron wanted to meet with some of these individuals once again and to study, as well, the viewing habits of current third graders. The documentary shows him exploring the views of children and adults and confirming the earlier research findings about the links between television viewing and higher levels of aggression.

Unfortunately, the lurid title of the *Frontline* program—"Does TV Kill?"—made it harder for reporters and viewers to sort out the evidence for such links. As a result, the greatest revelation turned out to be, for the reporters, not some new discovery about the role of television violence but rather, simply, "the stupefying amount that people watch."[6] It was only five decades ago that the first American families acquired their first television sets. By now, 98 percent of households have television, and a majority of children have sets in their bedrooms. The typical American household has the television set on for more than seven hours a day, and children ages two to eleven watch it on an average of three to four hours a day.[7]

Rip van Winkle might well find the children watching TV in their bedrooms and living rooms the most perplexing of all. If he watched *Frontline*, he would see a boy—one that psychologists would call an unusually heavy viewer—stretched on his bed in his own room, eyes trained on his TV set, day after day, sometimes taking time out only for brief meals, fidgeting, changing position, but absorbed in his viewing. Other children were filmed coming in and out of darkened living rooms, the screen flickering before their eyes, their faces mostly expressionless, at times half-excited or turned away in fear.

How to explain to anyone not familiar with the role of television today these children's passivity, their remaining indoors for hours on end, their absorbed silence? Or the American Heart Association's 1992 poster: CAUTION: CHILDREN NOT AT PLAY, warning of the health risks from too much passive viewing?[8]

Most troubling of all might be the chill realization that the children in the *Frontline* documentary were doing what they actually thought they preferred to do. At the close of the program, a young boy, standing with his father and mother, is asked what he would say to someone offering him one million dollars on the condition that he never watch the television screen again. His instant reply: "I wouldn't do it." "Not even for a million dollars?" his mother asks incredulously. "Not even for a million." "Why?" Again an instant retort, as if the answer were self-evident: "What [else] would you do?"

Anyone who had written on the subject of education and child-rearing before the advent of TV, from Aristotle and Rousseau to Dewey, Montessori, and Piaget would be hard put to explain what would cause a child to give up so many activities and to refuse a fortune in order not to be deprived of television. However much these thinkers differed about what sort of child-rearing is needed for individuals and societies to thrive, such a preference would jar with each of their views. Likewise, those who fought to establish the United States of America or who endured hardship to come to this nation as immigrants, however varied their own educational ideals and their hopes for their descendants, would surely be taken aback to learn how so many among today's children have been led to envisage "the pursuit of Happiness."

To be sure, many children in previous societies were much more deprived of opportunities to develop their full potential than the American youngsters studied by Eron. But it is odd that we in the twentieth century should pride ourselves on having arrived at a more enlightened view of children than the previous perception of them as "miniature adults," even as we acquiesce in having our own children targeted, long before the age of consent, as "miniature consumers."[9]

When Aldous Huxley looked back in 1958 at his novel *Brave New World*, written in 1931, he noted that some of the nefarious changes he had projected for a distant future were manifesting themselves much sooner, especially with respect to children. He warned of the growing powers of the communications industry in catering to what previous thinkers had ignored—"man's almost infinite appetite for distractions"—and in seeing children, especially, as offering lucrative prospects if they could be enlisted at an early age as lifelong consumers:

> They are ignorant of the world and its ways, and therefore completely unsuspecting. Their critical faculties are undeveloped. The youngest one of them have not yet reached the age of reason and the older ones lack the experience on which their newfound rationality can effectively work. In Europe, conscripts used to be playfully referred to as "cannon fodder." Their little brothers and sisters have now become radio fodder and television fodder.[10]

Huxley was referring to television and radio in general, not to violent programming in particular. His condemnation is too slashing to do justice to the extraordinary opportunities for creativity, learning, and enjoyment that modern media were already then capable of providing. It is important to go beyond such blanket indictments as we consider screen violence in the larger context of the media; and to keep in mind that in homes where television sets are on most of the time, whether or not anyone watches them, much programming may serve as background "wallpaper" with few measurable effects of any kind.

There is nevertheless widespread agreement that television habits can be harmful. But as many investigators point out, it is not easy to sort out how different causal factors interact. It is even harder to pinpoint the precise neurological pathway of any one factor as it influences the others. For this reason, while most studies of the relationship between viewing patterns and, say, health or school performance speak of the "effects" of television, they also make clear that they have in mind some form of correlation rather than some direct cause-effect relationship.

Does this mean that all talk of effects can be set aside as unreliable until the firmest scientific evidence is in hand? No—no more than talk of the effects of tobacco, say, or of malnutrition. An approach to causation that helps make sense of the language of effects even before absolute physiological proof is in hand is that of "probabilistic causation." According to this perspective, it is not necessary that a suspected risk—such as cigarette smoking—produce the designated effect—lung cancer—in all or even most cases, nor that it be the only or the greatest cause of that effect. Rather, it is thought to have an effect if it "increases the incidence of the effect for a population and increases the likelihood of the effect in an individual case."[11] It is from this perspective that I shall be considering the different studies of the effects of media exposure.

Sitting too long in front of a screen proves both physically and psychologically debilitating, no matter how innocuous or even beneficial the programs may be. The most basic physical needs of children, such as those of developing healthy hearts and lungs, are directly endangered by too many hours spent in front of television or computer screens. The more time children spend in front of the TV set, the more likely they are to be overweight and in poor physical condition.[12] On these scores, the American Heart Association, the American Academy of Pediatrics, and many other groups concerned with children's well-being unite in cautioning parents.[13]

In addition to physical risks from prolonged exposure to television, evidence is growing that it has harmful influences in other areas of life. Not unexpectedly, television watching has been found to cut back on time spent outdoors and on sports. Increasingly, now that most homes have several sets and many children have sets in their own rooms, it also isolates viewers. The time spent by parents with their children has continued to dwindle; a 1992 study shows that children have lost ten to twelve hours per week of parental time compared with 1960.[14] For beleaguered parents, television has come to seem a ready-made replacement for family interaction, storytelling, and supervision.[15] Studies have also linked sexually suggestive television programs with adolescent sexual behavior and out-of-wedlock pregnancy, as well as ads for beer and wine with increased alcohol consumption and greater incidence of accidents, drunk driving, and violence.[16]

When it comes to the relationship between viewing habits and schoolwork, opinions diverge. Does television expose children to learning opportunities they might not otherwise have, or does it interfere with their creativity, schoolwork, and reading ability? While heavy viewing is correlated with poorer performance in school and lower reading ability, both may be linked in the first place to the lower intellectual ability that is also associated with heavy television viewing, rather than to the viewing itself.[17]

Once young people go to college, their viewing habits have been found to correlate with lesser participation in activities in which they might otherwise engage. According to educational researchers Linda Sax and Alexander Astin, "the only measure to produce strong and negative effects on 'citizen development' among students, including leadership skills, cultural awareness, and tutoring other students, is more time spent watching television"; they have also found "uniformly negative effects of watching television [on] . . . college grades, self-reported growth in most areas of academic and personal development, and nearly all aspects of satisfaction with college."[18]

Given the variety of screen offerings now available from infancy on up and their impact, for better or worse, on health and well-being, much rides on the choices that parents make for children, and on those that older children and adolescents learn to make for themselves. The pediatrician and media consultant Milton Chen argues that it is as important to make informed choices about TV diet as to select balanced, nutritive foods.[19] And Elizabeth Thoman, director of the Center for Media Literacy, likewise stresses the importance of managing one's media diet, "that is, making choices and managing the amount of time spent with television, videos, electronic games, films, and various print media forms."[20]

While children and young people are more vulnerable in these respects, no age guarantees immunity to the different sorts of damage. And as with all consumption, viewing intake can be harmful in two ways. It may either simply displace activities needed for adequate for growth and sustenance, or else be actively toxic, at times addictive. It is in this context that questions concerning media violence enter in. Too much of *any* passive "consuming" of entertainment, even of the finest programs, damages children's health by taking away opportunities for sports and play and creative activities and the give-and-take of reciprocal engagement with others; but what has increasingly concerned parents and researchers is whether the consumption and enjoyment of media *violence* has additional and uniquely damaging effects.

SIZING UP THE
EFFECTS

A great deal of research has been conducted to sort out the kinds and amounts of violence in the media and to learn how exposure to media violence affects viewers, and especially children. There have also been many meta-analyses, or studies *of* existing studies.[21] Focusing primarily on television, they all confirm the commonsense observation that the screen is a powerful teaching medium, for good and for ill, when it comes to violent as to all other material.

There is general agreement that children ought neither to be insulated from gradual acquaintance with the treatment of violence in art and in the media nor assaulted by material they cannot handle. The *"catharsis* theory" put forth in the 1960s and 1970s, to the effect that violent material can help young people live out their aggressive impulses vicariously so that their day-to-day conduct becomes less aggressive, has been abandoned by almost all scholars in the field today.[22] The debate suffers, however, from the fact that different studies concern persons of different ages with different levels of understanding of the nature of violence and of distinctions between real and fictitious events. It seems reasonable to suppose that screen violence offers some viewers a chance for strictly vicarious role-playing and an outlet for aggressive fantasies, just as others are more easily frightened or mesmerized or incited by what they view. But scholars increasingly dismiss as unfounded any categorical claims that the average heavy viewer of media violence is somehow less likely to be aggressive than someone without such exposure.

Instead, the vast majority of the studies now concur that media violence can have both short-term and long-term debilitating effects. In 1993, the American Psychological Association published a report by a commission appointed to survey and review existing studies. According to this report,

> There is absolutely no doubt that higher levels of viewing violence on television are correlated with increased acceptance of aggressive attitudes and increased aggressive behavior. . . . Children's exposure to violence in the mass media, particularly at young ages, can have harmful lifelong consequences. Aggressive habits learned early in life are the foundation for later behavior. Aggressive children who have trouble in school and in relating to peers tend to watch more television; the violence they see there, in turn, reinforces their tendency toward aggression, compounding their academic and social failure. These effects are both short-term and long-lasting: A longitudinal study of boys found a significant relation between exposure to television violence at 8 years of life and anti-social acts—including serious violent criminal offenses and spouse abuse—22 years later. . . . In addition to increasing violent behaviors toward others, viewing violence on television changes attitudes and behaviors toward violence in significant ways. Even those who do not themselves increase their violent behaviors are significantly affected by their viewing of violence in three [further] ways:
> • Viewing violence increases fear of becoming a victim of violence, with a resultant increase in self-protective behaviors and increased mistrust of others;

- Viewing violence increases desensitization to violence, resulting in calloused attitudes toward violence directed at others and a decreased likelihood to take action on behalf of the victim when violence occurs (behavioral apathy); and
- Viewing violence increases viewers' appetites for becoming involved with violence or exposing themselves to violence.[23]

The report, like most of the research it surveys, speaks of viewing violence as correlated with effects rather than as directly causing them. And it specifies a number of risk factors capable of contributing to the first of these effects—increasing aggression. Among these risk factors, some, such as access to firearms, substance abuse, and experience of abuse as a child, doubtless play a larger role than media violence.[24] But it is on the screen that, as in no earlier generation, today's children, including those not subject to the other risk factors, become familiar with them all and with graphic depictions of every form of mayhem.

Commentators have spoken of the four effects specified in the report as increased aggression, fear, desensitization, and appetite.[25] Psychologist Ronald Slaby, a member of the APA commission, has named them "the aggressor effect, the victim effect, the bystander effect, and the appetite effect."[26] Not all of these effects, he suggests, occur for all viewers; much depends on how they identify themselves in relation to the violence they see and on their ability to evaluate programs critically.

Without taking such variations into account, it is natural to ask, as does critic John Leonard, "How, anyway, does TV manage somehow to *desensitize* but also *exacerbate*, to *sedate* but also *incite?*"[27] As with other stimuli, individuals react to media violence in different ways. While many people experience the quite natural reactions of fear and numbing when exposed to repeated depictions of assault, homicide, or rape, fewer will ever come close to feeling incited by them, much less to engaging in such acts. But among those who do cross that line, the combination of a surge of aggression and numb pitilessness is surely not unusual. Psychiatrist James Gilligan, in a study of homicidally violent men, takes it as a precondition for their being able to engage in violent behavior that ordinary human responses are absent: "What is most startling about the most violent people is how incapable they are, at least at the time they commit their violence, of feeling love, guilt, or fear."[28] In such a state, Macbeth's words are anything but incongruous:

> I am in blood
> Stepp'd in so far that, should I wade no more,
> Returning were as tedious as go o'er.[29]

As research evidence accumulates about the effects linked to media violence, it reinforces the commonsense view that violent programming influences viewers at least as much as the advertising directed at them for the express purpose of arousing their desire for candy and toys. Both types of exposure affect children most strongly to the degree that they are more suggestible and less critical of what is placed before them, and have more time to watch than most. The American Academy of Pediatrics, the American Medical Association, and the National PTA are among the many organizations signaling such effects and calling for reduced levels of television violence and greater parental involvement with children's viewing.

In the early 1990s, researchers frequently mentioned the estimate that the average child leaving elementary school has watched 8,000 murders and more than 100,000 acts of violence.[30] Because network television was for decades the primary source for screen violence in most homes, its role has been especially carefully charted in this regard. In recent years, growing access to numerous cable channels has brought in considerably more violent fare and made it available at all hours. By now, the vast assortment of slasher and gore films on video contribute to a climate of media violence different from that studied over the past four decades. So does the proliferation of video games offering players the chance to engage in vicarious carnage of every sort. These sources bring into homes depictions of graphic violence, often sexual in nature, never available to children and young people in the past. Because videos and interactive games also provide opportunities to play sequences over and over, they add greatly to the amount of violence to which viewers now have access. As a result, it may well be necessary to revise the earlier figures sharply upward.

Although most of the public's concern has been directed primarily toward the first of the four effects noted by researchers—increased levels of aggression—the other three may have a more widespread and debilitating impact on adults as well as children. After all, even in a high-crime society such as ours, the vast majority of citizens will never commit violent crimes; but many are still affected to the extent that the prominence of violence in news and entertainment programs brings an intensified fear of crime, greater callousness toward suffering, and a greater craving for ever more realistic entertainment violence.

In examining studies of the four types of effects, I shall therefore first take up those having to do with fear, desensitization, and appetite, before considering what we know about any links to aggression; and ask under what conditions each may inhibit the development of four basic moral characteristics—resilience, empathy, self-control, and respect for self and others—indispensable for human thriving.

FEAR

"Who killed him?" asked the four-year-old girl when her parents told her of the death of her playmate's father. The parents were prepared to discuss the many concerns that a child might have about the death of a parent, but not the question that she asked. After explaining that her playmate's father had died of a disease, they asked why she thought that someone had killed him. "Isn't that the way people die?" the girl asked. "That's the way people die on TV."

RONALD G. SLABY, "COMBATING TELEVISION VIOLENCE"[31]

With murder a commonplace on home screens, the little girl's question seems entirely reasonable. Television characters maim, torture, rape, and kill at a rate many times higher than people in real life.[32] Most children have witnessed many thousands more deaths on the screen than they have heard of in their own communities. When the screen barrage of crime, murder, and catastrophe generates an exaggerated view of the dangers surrounding them, it can intensify the fear that is a natural response to threatening information. Exposure to media violence is often singled out as among the factors contributing to the heightened fearfulness, depression, and pessimism that affect a far greater proportion of children and young people today than in the past.

Studies show that the sense that threats abound in the outside world is common among heavy TV viewers of all ages. Media expert George Gerbner, one of the first to study the risks from exposure to television violence, describes this effect as the "mean-world" syndrome: "Our analysis has found that exposure to violence-laden television cultivates an exaggerated sense of insecurity and mistrust, and anxiety about the mean world seen on television."[33] In Gerbner's view, increased aggression and the other debilitating effects of heavy media exposure matter, but less so than stronger feelings of vulnerability, which affect so much higher a percentage of viewers. He and his colleagues have found that "heavy viewers," those who watch television more than three hours a day, are more likely than "light viewers," exposed to two hours or less, to feel at high risk of victimization from violence, take their neighborhoods to be unsafe, and regard the world as "mean and gloomy."[34]

Newscasts play as large a role in the increased sense of fear as entertainment violence. The sense of threat is augmented by the fact that murder strikes victims more randomly now than in the past. Since 1960, murders of strangers have escalated from insignificant numbers to over a quarter of the nation's homicides in the 1990s.[35] The media, in turn, have dwelt to a vastly disproportionate degree on rare forms of violence such as serial killing, terrorism, and kidnapping. Instant and long-continued media coverage of the most shocking crime stories, such as the murders of Nicole Brown Simpson and Ronald Goldman and that of JonBenet Ramsey, add to the sense of dread about the dangers "out there" and help explain why a majority of Americans wrongly believe that crime is uniquely high and rising in the United States. Children are especially frightened by news stories relating horrors that have befallen other children.[36]

Kidnapping stories in particular strike at the heart of such fears. A story such as the 1993 kidnapping and murder of twelve-year-old Polly Klaas, in Petaluma, California, reverberates across the country, leaving children anxious about it for months and parents everywhere fearful for their family's safety. In a study of the media's coverage of that crime, psychiatrist Sara Stein found that about 80 percent of the children interviewed two months later either couldn't stop thinking or dreaming about the crime or were trying desperately to avoid thinking about it.[37] Historian Paula Fass cites a 1996 Roper poll showing that American children now fear being kidnapped as their "number one concern."[38] This can come as no surprise, she suggests, given the disproportionate and sensationalized media coverage in which child kidnapping both frightens and entertains us:

> As a society, we are haunted everywhere by pictures of abducted children in police stations, in newspapers, on television and posters, and on more homey objects like milk cartons. . . . By exploiting our fears and indulging our most extreme (and brutal) fantasies, our public representations . . . substitute thrill for social commitment.[39]

Kidnap stories, Fass holds, have haunted middle-class families far more than the dangers of neglect, abuse, and disadvantage that are so much more common in our children's lives. Psychologist James Garbarino has written of the "socially toxic" environment in which many American children now live, and of inner city children growing up in "war zones."[40] For millions of American children, the simple, age-old injunction to "go outside to play" is a thing of the past.[41] Some parents keep their children indoors in "lockdown" rather than allow them outside in the streets or the neighborhood parks and playgrounds. Many work long hours and find television viewing at home to be safer for their children than the risks outside the home: bullies in the streets, older friends luring them to consume or peddle drugs, strangers with evil designs, opportunities to get into trouble. As one ten-year-old put it:

> I used to hang out with my friends after school. Most of the time, we just acted stupid on the corner but that got dangerous and our moms said to quit it and come home. In this city, wear

your hat the wrong way and you are dead. Now, I go home and watch TV and sleep. I get scared all by myself, even though Mom says there's nothing to be afraid of in the day.

I would make a place for kids called My Father's Home. It would be a love place where's there's no killing. They'd have stuff for me to do. Lift weights, eat snacks, play games. . . .

I'd have beds at My Father's Home, like in a dormitory. Kids could sleep there in the summer when people go crazy on the streets. Last year, Mama and me slept on the floor, praying not to get shot.[42]

Fear, poverty, killings on the streets, and severe cutbacks in school, church, and community after-school programs make TV watching one of the few remaining "safe" activities for too many children like this boy. A vicious cycle can easily build up in this context: Since TV watching is thought to be safer than going outdoors, people stay indoors more and watch more TV; they may then in turn become more convinced of the risks on the outside, so they stay inside still more and watch still more TV.

That family life might fray under such circumstances is hardly a surprise. Community life, as well, is undercut. When a neighborhood is in the grip of fear, it becomes more difficult for people to help out with shared activities, arrange fairs, find adults to supervise athletic events, and attend evening meetings. Collective action to deal with shared problems suffers correspondingly, and TV watching becomes one of the few entertainment options left. Because disadvantaged youngsters in poor urban communities watch more TV than other children, they are more likely to experience fear and vulnerability, especially if violence in their own families or neighborhoods corroborates what they see on the screen.

Some children are more severely frightened by screen violence than parents expect. As one twelve-year-old boy described his reactions to a film: "It was a really gross movie and there's parts of it where they wrap bodies in foil and then light it on fire, you know, and then I got a lot of scary things like that and I get a lot of scary nightmares."[43]

Sometimes parents also worry about fears that never materialize.[44] This is more likely to be the case with subtle psychological violence rather than outright carnage. Most often, however, studies indicate that parents either fail to anticipate or even to notice their children's fright responses to mass media, and that "enduring, and sometimes severe emotional disturbances occur in a substantial proportion of children."[45]

A measure of fear and caution is necessary for purposes of survival and for navigating among real dangers in ordinary life. But emotional disturbances such as persistent nightmares, depression, irritability, inability to concentrate, and hypervigilance at sounds or motions that might constitute a threat go far beyond normal needs for such caution. We do not yet know to what degree exposure to violent programming may account for the rapid increase in psychological problems among children in recent decades. In his book *The Optimistic Child*, psychologist Martin Seligman notes that the levels of depression among adolescents have increased tenfold since the 1950s; and suicide rates for adolescents have tripled in the past three decades.[46] Even among youngsters aged fourteen or younger, suicide rates have increased by 75 percent in the past decade alone.[47]

Especially severe emotional disturbances are found in reactions to trauma known as post-traumatic stress disorder (PTSD).[48] Research has shown that children can be traumatized, not only by being treated violently but also by witnessing abuse in their homes or neighborhoods.[49] Given that small children cannot fully distinguish between violence witnessed in "real life" and on the TV screen, it is important to consider the risk that children will be traumatized by what they witness on their home screens.[50]

We are only on the threshold of research with respect to the effects of repeated or prolonged trauma on the brain. Neuroscientists are investigating how brain patterns and hormonal changes are related to symptoms such as hypervigilance, irritability, and difficulty concentrating.[51] There is no doubt, however, that excessive fear undercuts resilience, the ability to bounce back, to resist and overcome adversity—a characteristic very unevenly distributed, from earliest years on.[52] Just as researchers have long studied "risk factors" when it comes to resilience, so they are also increasingly considering "protective factors" and ways to enhance these. Drs. Roberta J. Apfel and Bennett Simon list, among traits contributing to resilience: resourcefulness, or the gift of being able to extract even very small amounts of human warmth in the most dire of circumstances and of knowing how to attract and use adult support outside the family if they cannot find it in their own family; curiosity, intellectual mastery, and the ability to relate one's own difficulties to others and to empathize with, say, seriously disturbed parents while keeping a safe distance and knowing how to find a safe place; a flexible array of emotional defenses including the ability to laugh even in the most trying circumstances and the possibility of delaying crying until a safer time; some goal for which to live; and models, among adults, of helpfulness to others along with instruction in how to do likewise.[53]

Apfel and Simon mention that Lebanese children in war-torn Beirut, whose mothers instructed them to go out, in the intervals between shellings, to bring food to an invalid relative, instead of hovering at home watching television, fared much better psychologically. These children benefited from having models of empathy for the distress of others and of courage under stress, as well as from being given opportunities to be of active help: "Maternal competence and altruism were strongly associated with children being relatively symptom-free under conditions of quite severe stress and danger."[54]

Other students of resilience include further factors that promote it, such as a sunny disposition, an exceptional teacher, a safe neighborhood, good after-school programs, and musical, athletic, or other talents. Each can make a difference in a child's life, no matter how beleaguered. But all agree that an essential ingredient is a capacity for empathy and fellow-feeling and a disposition to be of help to others— something not merely good and admirable in its own right but also often necessary for thriving, and even for survival under adverse conditions.

DESENSITIZATION

Two generations ago only a few unfortunate children ever saw any one hit over the head with a brick, shot, rammed by a car, blown up, immolated, raped or tortured. Now all children, along with their elders, see such images every day of their lives and are expected to enjoy them. . . . The seven-year-old who hides his eyes in the family cops-and-robbers drama is desensitized four years later to a point where he crunches potato chips through the latest video nasty.

PENELOPE LEACH, *CHILDREN FIRST*[55]

What Leach describes is the instinctive, utterly natural self-shielding against anxiety provoked by experiences that could otherwise be overwhelming.[56] From infancy on, our reflexes protect us from being overwhelmed by the masses of sensory impressions and images that surround us. Had we no such protection, we would be exposed to far more stimulation than we could cope with even at the most primitive sensory basis: it would be like being without skin. Gradually, we also learn to shield our emotions more selectively from the full impact of scenes and from knowledge that might otherwise be too painful.

It is therefore only to be expected that research should show children and adults guarding against media violence in the ways described by Leach. The need for such self-shielding has grown in recent decades, with more violent scenes available on more channels and over more types of media in more homes. Both news and entertainment programs motivate viewers to guard against the full impact of what they witness; but newscasts do so more directly, by dwelling on actual instances of murder, terrorism, and warfare from every corner of the world, repeating the most shocking scenes by the hour. Columnist Max Frankel describes viewing forty-eight hours of local news in New York City at a time when local events failed to "supply enough depravity" and the stations imported more by satellite or syndicate:

> In one 48-hour period that offered only modest local criminality, viewers had to suffer bulletins on every channel about a woman, conveniently cast as a "model," missing in California and another, dubbed an "heiress," missing in Mississippi. We saw the killing of a tiger who had mauled a 3-year-old in South Carolina, the rampage of highway bandits along the Mexican border, a mob's machete assault on a crook in Thailand and the lynching of a bank robber in Brazil. It was also a poor couple of days for disasters nearby, so we were subjected to scenes of: 1) "leptospirosis injury" in Nicaragua, a bleeding into the lungs caused by a "central American bacterium" that "is coming our way"; 2) an overturned bus in Maryland in which five persons died; and 3) bits of debris from the crash of a single-engine plane into an apartment building, killing three in Fullerton, Calif.[57]

No one can possibly supply enough genuine compassion for all the victims of all the disasters and epidemics and crimes witnessed on the screen. The multitudes of victims blur in many people's minds, the more so if they feel unable to imagine how they might be of help to even a few sufferers. The result can be what has come to be called "compassion fatigue," a state of mind that makes it possible to view violence as an uninvolved bystander.

Such compassion fatigue is often premature; but for individuals feeling bombarded by information about murder and mayhem, a measure of desensitization may be an increasingly indispensable psychological survival skill to avoid debilitating anxiety. Indeed, one form of therapy for persons suffering from pathological fears consists precisely in exposing them repeatedly to the situations provoking their fears so that they can gradually become desensitized to these situations and overcome the anxiety that has bedeviled them in the first place.[58]

Might we conclude, by analogy, that desensitization in response to media violence is not only not harmful but actually helps to counteract the fear and anxiety that such violence might otherwise provoke? Could it be that the psychologists and parents who express concern about such numbing should regard it, instead, as a valuable mechanism for psychological survival in today's media world? Such a conclusion might be warranted if it were possible to insulate the effects of media violence from the rest of life—to so compartmentalize experience that the numbing of feeling through exposure to brutality and suffering on the screen would not risk spilling over to similar scenes in real life. But such full compartmentalization is not possible even for adults, much less for children. As a result, it is important to ask to what degree desensitization may shrink empathy for suffering in real life and diminish the readiness to go to the help of persons in need.

It is this question that underlies the concept of the "bystander effect." Are viewers of television violence who demonstrate this effect not only desensitized in the most general way but also "more likely than other people to be callous toward victims of violence and to be apathetic toward others who engage in violence"?[59] On this score, there is disagreement among investigators. According to psychologist Aletha Huston, a 1986 study of the effects of viewing violent television demonstrates that children and adults who are exposed to such violence "are less likely than unexposed individuals to seek help for victims of violence."[60] Linda Heath and colleagues, on the other hand, in surveying the limited studies available through the late 1980s, found no evidence that media violence causes callousness in children.[61]

More research is needed, therefore, to determine more specifically when, if ever, media violence produces not just "compassion fatigue" but callousness in real-life situations. In this respect, entertainment violence may play a special role, along with news reporting when it is exploited for entertainment purposes, as in many contemporary "infotainment" programs. To the extent that people seek out violent programming for the enjoyment and the excitement that the violence itself can provide, they may run a higher risk of suppressing empathy—the crucial ability to feel with and for others and to respond to their suffering.

Empathy and fellow feeling form the very basis of morality, as philosophers as different as Mencius and Immanuel Kant have maintained.[62] Without some rudimentary perception of the needs and feelings of others, there can be no beginnings of felt responsibility toward them. Developing the capacity for such perception is aided by the gaze of infants at the eyes of the person nursing them and by the experience of bonding and reciprocity. For psychologist Jerome Kagan,

> The two year old has a capacity to infer the thoughts and feelings of another and will show signs of tension if another person is hurt or will offer penance if she causes another's distress. As a result, an intention to hurt another leads to an anticipation of the unpleasant feelings the other might experience—that is, empathy—and to suppression of the asocial act.[63]

The development of empathy, Kagan suggests, is followed, not long after, by the ability to feel guilt for having caused distress and the impulse to offer help to others. The capacities for empathy, for feeling responsibility toward others, and for reaching out to help them can be stunted or undermined early on, depending on a child's experiences in the home and neighborhood. Cultures the world over stress the need to reinforce these capacities, and the indispensable role, not only of seeing to children's need for adequate bodily nourishment but of the form of nurturing that is often called civilizing, socializing, or humanizing, performed by families, communities, and schools.

Not all are as pessimistic about the prospects for such nurturing as John Stuart Mill, who held that the capacity for the nobler feelings "is in most natures a very tender plant, easily killed, not only by hostile influences, but by mere want of sustenance."[64] But all agree that both physical and psychological nurturing are closely linked and that no child can thrive on either one alone. Children who are neglected or abused or otherwise deprived of psychological nurturance can be well developed physically and mentally, yet lag behind in what one might call moral growth, using the term "moral" in the sense of both ethical and emotional growth.[65]

The risks are greatest for children who have been most severely deprived of the care, support, and guidance they need to develop the most basic sense of reciprocity with respect to others and, gradually, a secure sense of self as relating to others. Such children may suffer from a psychological "failure to thrive," analogous to the physical failure to thrive diagnosed among some infants.[66] T. Berry Brazelton, the pediatrician, writes of wizened eight-month-old babies who still weigh the same as they did at birth; even though they may have been given enough food, loving communication has been lacking: "By the time they are admitted to the hospital, their faces are hopelessly unresponsive, their eyes are dull, they look past caregivers, and they can't communicate."[67]

Among children who exhibit the arrested growth, pallor, and wasting characteristic of the nutritional "failure to thrive" syndrome, some suffer primarily from such neglect; others have experienced overwhelming trauma. Many children are remarkably resilient in the face even of severe injuries and neglect: only a small percentage fall into the category where such failure to thrive is diagnosed. The comparable psychological condition characterizes children with an especially underdeveloped, wizened understanding of self and others, inadequate responses of respect, inability to experience empathy or pity. Many factors contribute to such psychological failure to thrive, just as with the physical condition. In both instances, parental neglect and abuse play a role, as do trauma and psychological stress both from witnessing and from being subjected to abuse and other injuries.[68]

When might media violence, and especially entertainment vio-

lence, be most likely to counteract the normal development of resilience and empathy among children? The children most heavily
exposed to such violence are at greatest risk when they are deprived of
adequate parental empathy, nurturance, and guidance. And to the
extent that the suffering they witness on- and offscreen blurs, as is the
case for young children living with abusive family members, the
bystander effect is still more likely to spread from one realm to the
other.

Does media violence pose similar risks to adolescents and adults?
Even though they are more capable of distinguishing the two realms,
their own evaluation of what is and is not violent may have been
affected over time by such exposure, making it easier for them to take a
passive bystander's attitude to witnessing aggression and the infliction
of pain. For example, research on college-age men who view films
portraying violence against women suggests that the viewers became
increasingly comfortable with the violent content of the films, eventu-
ally considering it less offensive and degrading to the victims and the
films less violent than they had initially thought.[69] One investigator
advances the hypothesis, as he looks back with colleagues at such
research, that the "altered perceptual and affective reactions may then
be carried over into judgments made about victims in other, more
realistic settings."[70]

A growing proportion of young adults appear to perceive nothing problematic about TV violence. A 1993 Times Mirror survey
concludes that there is a "video violence" generation gap: "Those
under 30 are far more likely to be heavy consumers of violent
programming and movies. [They] are far less bothered by violence
on television, less likely to feel violence is harmful to society than are
older Americans."[71] This difference in the attitudes of young adults
may be due in part to the fact that many of them have not yet had
children themselves and so have not had reason to try to put themselves in the place of a child exposed to today's levels of entertainment violence. But the difference may also result from cumulative
desensitization. Young adults have been more massively exposed to
this influence than their elders, starting at a younger age. If so, then

the generation gap may well shift upward in age as more and more cohorts of children grow up having been exposed to heavy doses of media violence.

Media critics may be the most heavily exposed consumers of such violence, along with children, invalids, and prisoners; among them, critics alone have to sit through offerings they might otherwise reject, to do their job of evaluating and advising the public. Reporter Betsy Sherman describes the numbing that can result:

> As a professional moviegoer, I see dozens of simulated killings
> per week. Some of the mayhem involves what we glibly call
> "cartoonish" violence. . . . Some of it is stylized violence, with a
> hail of machine-gun bullets producing aesthetically arranged
> fake-blood patterns. But much of it is violence-with-
> consequences, in the face of which we are meant to feel the
> pain of the victim or a survivor close to the victim. Me, I can
> sit and eat a sandwich while watching just about any of
> this. . . . I suspect that I have paid for my near-immunity to
> simulated violence by heightened levels of anxiety, paranoia,
> and guilt.[72]

Critics vary in the degree to which they struggle against the near-immunity of which Betsy Sherman speaks. Some may believe that they must accept this effect from heavy exposure to media violence in order to do their job—a little as if they were soldiers or surgeons. The trouble is that the less empathy critics come to be able to muster for suffering, the more difficult it is for them to serve the needs of viewers less hardened than themselves. A few express acute discomfort at the prospect of any deadening of the emotions. According to critic Pauline Kael,

> It's the emotionlessness of so many violent movies that I'm
> becoming anxious about, not the rare violent movies (*Bonnie and*
> *Clyde, The Godfather, Mean Streets*) that make us care about the
> characters and what happens to them. A violent movie that
> intensifies our experience of violence is very different from a

movie in which acts of violence are perfunctory. I'm only guessing, and maybe this emotionlessness means little, but, if I can trust my instincts at all, there's something deeply wrong about anyone's taking for granted the dissociation that this carnage without emotion represents.[73]

Others find "carnage without emotion" necessary for a more refined "aestheticization" of the experience of violence. They have learned to fuse emotional anaesthesia with greater stimulation of sensory and intellectual appetites; and they may strive to deaden emotions such as pity or grief to make room for heightened appreciation for the artistry, creativity, and ingenuity with which filmmakers convey the beauty and poetry of killing and mutilation. Critic Sarah Kerr, in dissecting the way in which director Quentin Tarantino used violence for purposes of surprise and humor in *Pulp Fiction*, speaks of the effect of numbness, bordering on pathology, the film produces, and of the audience submitting to "a new kind of enthrallment . . . over and over again we were provoked into responding, but we didn't have to feel a thing."[74]

Learning "not to feel a thing" involves suppressing ordinary responses to the suffering of *others* and focusing instead on one's own visual, hormonal, and auditory sensations. In this respect, it chokes off empathy toward others in order to enhance unencumbered aesthetic pleasure, possibly stimulating an appetite for more frequent and more powerful experiences of this nature. People's attitudes toward such a learning process vary depending on their awareness of its effects, their degree of aversion to these effects, their capacity for empathy, the countervailing delight they have already come to experience from entertainment violence, and their ability to erect barriers between vicarious and real-life violence. But while adults have the opportunity to choose whether to take such risks, many children are exposed to media violence before they are capable of making such choices.

For critic David Denby, his own "personal calvary" in this respect came, he writes, after his twelve-year-old son saw and enjoyed *Pulp Fiction* as a "series of wicked thrills" at a friend's house without his permission, then wanted to go on to see Tarantino's "earlier and much nastier (and more pointless) 'Reservoir Dogs.'" Denby is not worried that his children will behave violently or turn to crime; rather, what he deplores are the effects of their numbing absorption in and by the media:

> The danger is not mere exposure to occasional violent or prurient images but the acceptance of a degraded environment that devalues everything—a shadow world in which our kids are breathing an awful lot of poison without knowing that there is clean air and sunshine elsewhere. They are shaped by the media as consumers before they've had a chance to develop their souls.[75]

I take the danger to the souls of children to which Denby points to arise not so much from experiences that "stab the soul," to use Saint Augustine's expression, as from immersion in an atmosphere that thwarts the spirit still earlier in life—something more akin to stifling than to wounding. Many children will doubtless be resilient enough to work their way out of that atmosphere—the more so if they have supportive parents or other adults aware of its effects. Without anyone to signal such dangers to what I think Denby is right to call "the chance to develop their souls," the risks of excessive desensitization are real and can bring about, in turn, a stifling of empathy and fellow feeling beyond the world of the screen. It is the stifling against which Rabindranath Tagore warned long before the age of modern media, in "A Poet's School":

> Apathy and ignorance are the worst forms of bondage for man; they are the invisible walls of confinement that we carry round us when we are in their grip. Our reasoning faculties have to be nourished in order to allow our mind its freedom in the world of truth, our imagination for the world which belongs to art, and our sympathy for the world of human relationship. This last is even more important than learning the geography of foreign lands.[76]

When might heavy or exceptionally shocking exposure to media violence do most to counter the development of empathy and reciprocity? Among the different effects of such exposure, increased fear and aggression serve to limit the scope of empathy to fewer persons, and desensitization, when it involves "learning not to feel a thing," weakens empathy overall. But it is the third effect, appetite for exposure to more violence and for higher levels of violence, that may do the greatest harm in this respect by throwing the development of empathy screeching into reverse.

APPETITE FOR
MORE VIOLENCE

"I've seen someone up close get shot in the head. I've seen just about any kind. I haven't seen anybody get shot in the eye. I've seen someone do this"—he puts a finger in his mouth and pretends to pull a trigger—"and you see blood come out the back of the head. I've seen people shot in the leg, shot in the back.

"And stabbings: In the back. In the stomach. Slice their neck. Scar their face. I don't think I've seen eyes gouged out. I've seen after, but I didn't see the process. I saw someone slit their wrists for a suicide. . . .

"I like violence," he says.

He elaborates: "I like seeing violence."

And elaborates further: "I just really like seeing violence."[77]

These are the words of a fourteen-year-old boy talking to an interviewer about films that he's seen and about some of the varieties of stabbings and shootings that he's enjoyed. He is described as passionate about violence in films, TV programs, and cutting-edge interactive computer games. He spends more than a hundred dollars a year at the arcade playing the latest versions of Mortal Kombat, for which he has learned moves such as the "head inflation," the "skull rip," and the "death scream." With his parents footing the bills, he spends far more than that on home versions of this and other games and on videos and movies. As parents of other youngsters attest, and as soaring sales figures for such games confirm, this boy's tastes are by no means unusual. It is their children's passionate involvement with violent programming along with their eerie lack of empathy toward suffering that causes growing numbers of parents to worry: Will these traits turn out to be lasting? And is there mutual reinforcement between this detachment and the actual enjoyment, the thrill in violence, the appetite for more, that its presentation as glamorous and empowering makes possible? The appetite is fanned by the glamorization of violence and energized whenever viewers identify with the aggressor or even carry out the aggression themselves in an interactive game.

Learning to laugh at the violence in programs such as *Mighty Morphin Power Rangers*—the most violent series of programs produced to date for young children—may condition the youngest viewers to later enjoyment of sadistic interactive games. On these programs, killing is fun, and jokes about killing are sharp and witty. "What a splitting headache he's gonna have," says a Power Ranger as he slices someone in two. Rangers are a group of attractive adolescent boys and girls from diverse ethnic groups, capable of "morphing" or transforming themselves into figures battling monsters and evil agents planning a world takeover. Invincible and invulnerable, the Rangers have a wide range of gruesome methods for dispatching their foes: by pulverizing them, exploding them, dismembering them, strangling them, burning them, or zapping them by means of shiny, ingenious weapons, all with elegance, agility, and breathtaking speed.

Such programs are popular even among two-to-three year olds. They sit absorbed in front of their sets, drinking in the color, glamour, energy of these programs, then attempt to execute the strokes and kicks of the Rangers on their own, often continuing to do so at playgrounds and in schoolyards. The series is marketed to hundreds of millions of children the world over, and its color, its movement, its exciting story lines generate near-hypnotic appeal for many. The shows are meant primarily as entertainment, but they turn out to be learning experiences as well, providing role models and teaching attitudes, expressions, postures, bodily moves. Above all, the programs induce children to be consumers, to want the costumes and toys that will allow them to "morph" into Power Rangers as mighty as those on the screen. The commercial sponsors of children's programs aim at increasing young viewers' appetites for their products, be they guns, cereals, candy, games, or other toys. But advertisers also take a longer view. Marketing expert James McNeal explains that "as U.S. marketers have known for a long time, and as large numbers of them have begun recently to act on, children are a future market that can be cultivated now so that when children reach market age they can more easily be converted into customers—hopefully into loyal customers."[78]

Children reach "market age" earlier than ever. By the time they are three, many youngsters beg and plead for products they have seen advertised on the screen, exercising vehement and commercially lucrative influence over family purchases. By the time they are a few years older, children acculturated in this way are capable of ostracizing children who are not. One mother, who, with her husband, limited TV viewing for their children, kept out all violent programming, and declined to purchase the associated games and weapons, told me of her distress at hearing her seven-year-old son's friends refuse to come to play at his house. The reason? "There's no killing there."

This boy's parents felt torn at the thought that their son could be isolated unless he could provide the type of entertainment at his house to which his playmates were accustomed. Many other parents are likewise concerned that their children will not be accepted unless they watch all the programs their friends talk about at school, but they are also troubled that even the youngest children can be induced to savor violence by media programming and marketing as well as by pressure from friends and playmates.

Why be concerned on that score? After all, the violence is only make-believe, only meant to be enjoyed "for fun." But many parents sense that there may be peril in inducing small children to take pleasure in cruelty and vice and that the peril may be of a moral nature.

Allowing them to become acculturated to such pleasures goes against their humanizing efforts to teach children to hold back on cruelty and violence, efforts that are basic to child-rearing and difficult enough to carry out as it is. None of us starts life able to exercise discrimination with respect to what we associate with pleasure, as Aristotle persuasively argued; we can be made worse by pursuing and avoiding the wrong pleasures and pains, which is why we need to have the right kind of upbringing from our earliest years, "to make us find enjoyment or pain in the right things."[79]

Some suggest a further danger from encouraging the appetite for violent entertainment: that this appetite, much like appetites for other activities found pleasurable, can turn into an addiction, characterized by higher and higher tolerance levels and by withdrawal symptoms for those who try to stop.[80] As it does with many other stimuli, the phenomenon known as "habituation" also operates when it comes to violence. The greater the level of detachment and numbing, the more of the stimulus is needed to bring about what marketing strategists call "arousal" and, in turn, to produce whatever pleasure the activity can bring. Neurological research is shedding new light on neural mechanisms by which stimulation affects viewers' appetites, and the processes leading from initial pleasure to attachment to reiteration and, finally to addiction.[81] We are learning more about how addiction differs from habits less likely to result in dependence, and about how age, heredity, outside supports, and maturity affect one's ability to exert self-control.

Violent interactive video games such as Carmageddon or Mortal Kombat may increase chances of addiction, since they can be replayed at will. In such games, the most pleasurable killings of pedestrians or opponents can not only be performed over and over, but be rewarded each time they are well executed. In one treatment center for addiction, a Swedish psychologist reports, so-called "game abusers" can get to the point of playing video games around the clock, reacting as vehemently to deprivation as alcoholics or other substance abusers.[82] Such extreme instances, he adds, are rare, and there are many constructive video games that present no such risks.

Regardless of how often the appetite for entertainment violence becomes addictive, increased exposure does risk further desensitizing viewers. And the element of pleasure that they derive may lead them to regard violence as a more acceptable way of dealing with problems and victimization as more tolerable so long as it befalls others, not themselves. We are then left with the question of whether the appetite for violence also makes it easier for some people to shift from enjoying it on the screen to resorting to it in real life.

AGGRESSION

Even if media violence were linked to no other debilitating effects, it would remain at the center of public debate so long as the widespread belief persists that it glamorizes aggressive conduct, removes inhibitions toward such conduct, arouses viewers, and invites imitation. It is only natural that the links of media violence to aggression should be of special concern to families and communities. Whereas increased fear, desensitization, and appetite primarily affect the viewers themselves, aggression directly injures others and represents a more clear-cut violation of standards of behavior. From the point of view of public policy, therefore, curbing aggression has priority over alleviating subtler psychological and moral damage.

Public concern about a possible link between media violence and societal violence has further intensified in the past decade, as violent crime reached a peak in the early 1990s, yet has shown no sign of downturn, even after crime rates began dropping in 1992. Media coverage of violence, far from declining, has escalated since then, devoting ever more attention to celebrity homicides and copycat crimes. The latter, explicitly modeled on videos or films and sometimes carried out with meticulous fidelity to detail, are never more relentlessly covered in the media than when they are committed by children and adolescents. Undocumented claims that violent copycat crimes are mounting in number contribute further to the ominous sense of threat that these crimes generate.[83] Their dramatic nature drains away the public's attention from other, more mundane forms of aggression that are much more commonplace, and from the other three harmful effects of media violence.

Media analyst Ken Auletta reports that, in 1992, a mother in France sued the head of a state TV channel that carried the American series *MacGyver*, claiming that her son was accidentally injured as a result of having copied MacGyver's recipe for making a bomb.[84] At the time, Auletta predicted that similar lawsuits were bound to become a weapon against media violence in America's litigious culture. By 1996, novelist John Grisham had sparked a debate about director Oliver Stone's film *Natural Born Killers*, which is reputedly linked to more copycat assaults and murders than any other movie to date.[85] Grisham wrote in protest against the film after learning that a friend of his, Bill Savage, had been killed by nineteen-year-old Sarah Edmondson and her boyfriend Benjamin Darras, eighteen: after repeated viewings of Stone's film on video, the two had gone on a killing spree with the film's murderous, gleeful heroes expressly in mind.[86] Characterizing the film as "a horrific movie that glamorized casual mayhem and bloodlust," Grisham proposed legal action:

> Think of a film as a product, something created and brought to market, not too dissimilar from breast implants. Though the law has yet to declare movies to be products, it is only a small step away. If something goes wrong with the product, either by design or defect, and injury ensues, then its makers are held responsible. . . . It will take only one large verdict against the likes of Oliver Stone, and his production company, and perhaps the screenwriter, and the studio itself, and then the party will be over. The verdict will come from the heartland, far away from Southern California, in some small courtroom with no cameras. A jury will finally say enough is enough; that the demons placed in Sarah Edmondson's mind were not solely of her own making.[87]

As a producer of books made into lucrative movies—themselves hardly devoid of violence—and as a veteran of contract negotiations within the entertainment industry, Grisham may have become accustomed to thinking of films in industry terms as "products." As a seasoned courtroom lawyer, he may have found the analogy between such products and breast implants useful for invoking product liability to pin personal responsibility on movie producers and directors for the lethal consequences that their work might help unleash.

Oliver Stone retorted that Grisham was drawing "upon the superstition about the magical power of pictures to conjure up the undead spectre of censorship."[88] In dismissing concerns about the "magical power of pictures" as merely superstitious, Stone sidestepped the larger question of responsibility fully as much as Grisham had sidestepped that of causation when he attributed liability to filmmakers for anything that "goes wrong" with their products so that "injury ensues."

Because aggression is the most prominent effect associated with media violence in the public's mind, it is natural that it should also remain the primary focus of scholars in the field. The "aggressor effect" has been studied both to identify the short-term, immediate impact on viewers after exposure to TV violence, and the long-term influences such as those studied by Dr. Eron and his colleagues in Hudson, New York. There is near-unanimity by now among investigators that exposure to media violence contributes to lowering barriers to aggression among some viewers. This lowering of barriers may be assisted by the failure of empathy that comes with growing desensitization, and intensified to the extent that viewers develop an appetite for violence—something that may lead to still greater desire for violent programs and, in turn, even greater desensitization.

When it comes to viewing violent pornography, levels of aggression toward women have been shown to go up among male subjects who they view sexualized violence against women. "In explicit depictions of sexual violence," a report by the American Psychological Association's Commission on Youth and Violence concludes after surveying available research data, "it is the message about violence more than the sexual nature of the materials that appears to affect the attitudes of adolescents about rape and violence toward women."[89] Psychologist Edward Donnerstein and colleagues have shown that if investigators tell subjects that aggression is legitimate, then show them violent pornography, their aggression toward women increases. In slasher films, the speed and ease with which "one's feelings can be transformed from sensuality into viciousness may surprise even those quite conversant with the links between sexual and violent urges."[90]

Viewers who become accustomed to seeing violence as an acceptable, common, and attractive way of dealing with problems find it easier to identify with aggressors and to suppress any sense of pity or respect for victims of violence. Media violence has been found to have stronger effects of this kind when carried out by heroic, impressive, or otherwise exciting figures, especially when they are shown as invulnerable and are rewarded or not punished for what they do. The same is true when the violence is shown as justifiable, when viewers identify with the aggressors rather than with their victims, when violence is routinely resorted to, and when the programs have links to how viewers perceive their own environment.[91]

While the consensus that such influences exist grows among investigators as research accumulates, there is no consensus whatsoever about the size of the correlations involved. Most investigators agree that it will always be difficult to disentangle the precise effects of exposure to media violence from the many other factors contributing to societal violence. No reputable scholar accepts the view expressed by 21 percent of the American public in 1995, blaming television more than any other factor for teenage violence.[92] Such tentative estimates as have been made suggest that the media account for between 5 and 15 percent of societal violence.[93] Even these estimates are rarely specific enough to indicate whether what is at issue is all violent crime, or such crimes along with bullying and aggression more generally.

One frequently cited investigator proposes a dramatically higher and more specific estimate than others. Psychiatrist Brandon S. Centerwall has concluded from large-scale epidemiological studies of "white homicide" in the United States, Canada, and South Africa in the period from 1945 to 1974, that it escalated in these societies within ten to fifteen years of the introduction of television, and that one can therefore deduce that television has brought a doubling of violent societal crime:

> Of course, there are many factors other than television that influence the amount of violent crime. Every violent act is the result of a variety of forces coming together—poverty, crime, alcohol and drug abuse, stress—of which childhood TV exposure is just one. Nevertheless, the evidence indicates that if, hypothetically, television technology had never been developed, there would today be 10,000 fewer homicides each year in the United States, 70,000 fewer rapes, and 700,000 fewer injurious assaults. Violent crime would be half of what it now is.[94]

Centerwall's study, published in 1989, includes controls for such variables as firearm possession and economic growth.[95] But his conclusions have been criticized for not taking into account other factors, such as population changes during the time period studied, that might also play a role in changing crime rates.[96] Shifts in policy and length of prison terms clearly affect these levels as well. By now, the decline in levels of violent crime in the United States since Centerwall's study was conducted, even though television viewing did not decline ten to fifteen years before, does not square with his extrapolations. As for "white homicide" in South Africa under apartheid, each year brings more severe challenges to official statistics from that period.

Even the lower estimates, however, of around 5 to 10 percent of violence as correlated with television exposure, point to substantial numbers of violent crimes in a population as large as America's. But if such estimates are to be used in discussions of policy decisions, more research will be needed to distinguish between the effects of television in general and those of particular types of violent programming, and to indicate specifically what sorts of images increase the aggressor effect and by what means; and throughout to be clearer about the nature of the aggressive acts studied.

Media representatives naturally request proof of such effects before they are asked to undertake substantial changes in programming. In considering possible remedies for a problem, inquiring into the reasons for claims about risks is entirely appropriate. It is clearly valid to scrutinize the research designs, sampling methods, and possible biases of studies supporting such claims, and to ask about the reasoning leading from particular research findings to conclusions. But to ask for some demonstrable pinpointing of just when and how exposure to media violence affects levels of aggression sets a dangerously high threshold for establishing risk factors.

We may never be able to trace, retrospectively, the specific set of television programs that contributed to a particular person's aggressive conduct. The same is true when it comes to the links between tobacco smoking and cancer, between drunk driving and automobile accidents, and many other risk factors presenting public health hazards. Only recently have scientists identified the specific channels through which tobacco generates its carcinogenic effects. Both precise causative mechanisms and documented occurrences in individuals remain elusive. Too often, media representatives formulate their requests in what appear to be strictly polemical terms, raising dismissive questions familiar from debates over the effects of tobacco: "How can anyone definitively pinpoint the link between media violence and acts of real-life violence? If not, how can we know if exposure to media violence constitutes a risk factor in the first place?"

Yet the difficulty in carrying out such pinpointing has not stood in the way of discussing and promoting efforts to curtail cigarette smoking and drunk driving. It is not clear, therefore, why a similar difficulty should block such efforts when it comes to media violence. The perspective of "probabilistic causation," mentioned earlier, is crucial to public debate about the risk factors in media violence.[97] The television industry has already been persuaded to curtail the glamorization of smoking and drunk driving on its programs, despite the lack of conclusive documentation of the correlation between TV viewing and higher incidence of such conduct. Why should the industry not take analogous precautions with respect violent programming?

Americans have special reasons to inquire into the causes of societal violence. While we are in no sense uniquely violent, we need to ask about all possible reasons why our levels of violent crime are higher than in all other stable industrialized democracies. Our homicide rate would be higher still if we did not imprison more of our citizens than any society in the world, and if emergency medical care had not improved so greatly in recent decades that a larger proportion of shooting victims survive than in the past. Even so, we have seen an unprecedented rise not only in child and adolescent violence, but in levels of rape, child abuse, domestic violence, and every other form of assault.[98]

Although America's homicide rate has declined in the 1990s, the rates for suicide, rape, and murder involving children and adolescents in many regions have too rarely followed suit. For Americans aged 15 to 34 years, homicide is the second leading cause of death, and for young African Americans, 15 to 24 years, it is *the* leading cause of death.[99] In the decade following the mid-1980s, the rate of murder committed by teenagers 14 to 17 more than doubled. The rates of injury suffered by small children are skyrocketing, with the number of seriously injured children nearly quadrupling from 1986 to 1993; and a proportion of these injuries are inflicted by children upon one another.[100] Even homicides by children, once next to unknown, have escalated in recent decades.

America may be the only society on earth to have experienced what has been called an "epidemic of children killing children," which is ravaging some of its communities today.[101] As in any epidemic, it is urgent to ask what it is that makes so many capable of such violence, victimizes so many others, and causes countless more to live in fear.[102] Whatever role the media are found to play in this respect, to be sure, is but part of the problem. Obviously, not even the total elimination of media violence would wipe out the problem of violence in the United States or any other society. The same can be said for the proliferation and easy access to guns, or for poverty, drug addiction, and other risk factors. As Dr. Deborah Prothrow-Stith puts it, "It's not an either or. It's not guns or media or parents or poverty."[103]

■   ■   ■

We have all witnessed the four effects that I have discussed in this chapter—fearfulness, numbing, appetite, and aggressive impulses—in the context of many influences apart from the media. Maturing involves learning to resist the dominion that these effects can gain over us; and to strive, instead, for greater resilience, empathy, self-control, and respect for self and others. The process of maturation and growth in these respects is never completed for any of us; but it is most easily thwarted in childhood, before it has had chance to take root. Such learning calls for nurturing and education at first; then for increasing autonomy in making personal decisions about how best to confront the realities of violence.

Today, the sights and sounds of violence on the screen affect this learning process from infancy on, in many homes. The television screen is the lens through which most children learn about violence. Through the magnifying power of this lens, their everyday life becomes suffused by images of shootings, family violence, gang warfare, kidnappings, and everything else that contributes to violence in our society. It shapes their experiences long before they have had the opportunity to consent to such shaping or developed the ability to cope adequately with this knowledge. The basic nurturing and protection to prevent the impairment of this ability ought to be the birthright of every child.

PART THREE

c e n s o r s h i p

The Revolution is like Saturn,
it eats its own children.

GEORG BÜCHNER, *DANTON'S DEATH*[1]

A PERCEIVED DILEMMA

Sooner or later censorship is going to have to be considered as popular culture continues plunging to ever more sickening lows. The alternative to censorship, legal and moral, will be a brutalized and chaotic culture, with all that entails for our society, economy, politics, and physical safety. ROBERT BORK, *SLOUCHING TOWARDS GOMORRAH*[2]

If we banned the expression of all ideas that might lead individuals to actions that might have an adverse impact even on important interests such as national security or public safety, then scarcely any idea would be safe and surely no idea that challenged the status quo would be. NADINE STROSSEN, *DEFENDING PORNOGRAPHY*[3]

Is it possible for societies to guard against the ill effects of media violence without inviting the evils that censorship can bring? Censorship, long the standard official response to writings and programs thought to be offensive or dangerous, is still exercised by religious and political authorities in most countries today. Even democracies with strong protections for political and religious freedom, such as Canada, Sweden, and Holland, have statutes limiting violent pornography and hate speech.

Most of the programming barred in those countries can be presented in the United States, where the First Amendment offers one of the world's strongest constitutional safeguards against censorship. But Americans divide sharply about the wisdom of such protection when it shelters speech that they find especially objectionable. Conservatives such as Judge Robert Bork advocate censorship by cutting back the power of the Supreme Court to enforce present protections for free speech; polls show more than one fifth of Americans agreeing that censorship is a legitimate response to what they see as media filth and brutality. At the other end of the spectrum of opinion, law professor Nadine Strossen speaks for civil libertarians and members of the entertainment industry and the world of letters, in warning against any move in the direction of stricter regulation.

Many advocates on each side are prepared to acknowledge the concerns raised on the other as legitimate, albeit outweighed by the arguments they put forth. But at both ends of the spectrum, purists reject all sense of conflict on this score. Religious fundamentalists striving to cleanse libraries, school curricula, and entertainment media regard their aims as outweighing any possible constitutional claims; likewise, those who call themselves First Amendment absolutists see no sacrifice as too great to make in defense of the freedoms that the Amendment protects. In both cases, advocates hold their views as articles of faith, whether religious or political, and as established beyond question in determinative texts such as the Bible and the U.S. Constitution. As a result, neither group sees the conflicting obligations concerning media violence as constituting a dilemma that requires further thought.

Between these two extremes are many people, perhaps a majority, who are more troubled. They find it harder to dismiss what does appear to them a moral dilemma: an obligation of responsibility to children and to society, on the one hand, and on the other, an obligation to safeguard rights fundamental to our democratic traditions. It seems impossible to act on both sets of obligations, yet equally difficult to renounce either one. The conviction that it would be wrong to act on either one of the obligations, but equally wrong to do nothing, leads to a sense of powerlessness and bewilderment. Too often, the result is either a conscious turning aside from the problem or a more inchoate moral paralysis about how best to respond.

The concern with the risks of media violence is warranted, I believe, for all the reasons given in Part Two. But the fear of any drift in the direction of censorship is surely also legitimate. In our century, we have witnessed efforts by theocracies and dictatorships to exert more ruthless and pervasive control over the media, the arts, and newscasts than was ever possible before. Officials in Nazi Germany could broadcast fabricated news reports, even as they provided escapist entertainment making no allusions to the unspeakable horrors that they were perpetrating.[4] In Maoist China, government secrecy and stranglehold over the media were largely to blame for the failure to report and take action against the great famine of 1959–61, which claimed more than 40 million lives. Even democracies, such as England and France, operate without anything like the First Amendment; and while this permits greater control over media violence and pornography, it also provides opportunities for political censorship.

In view of their legitimate desire to resist government inroads on free speech, one can understand the special tension Americans experience about how to respond to the acknowledged risks from media violence. But this tension is exacerbated by a misunderstanding of what constitutes censorship, especially a belief that not only restriction of speech by government but also the exercise of any sort of control or choice over expression amounts to censorship. Many hapless parents even imagine that limiting TV time at home amounts to censorship. The same expanded view permits media industry representatives to label as censorship almost any collective effort to counter media violence. Thus when a group of citizens organized a national "Turn Off the TV Day" in November 1992, the president of the Network Television Association objected, saying that "participating in national boycotts is an infringement of the networks' First Amendment Rights."[5]

To stretch the concept of censorship to include the rejection even of the private exercise of judgment and control over what is spoken and heard risks short-circuiting policy debate.[6] The First Amendment concerns restriction of speech by government, not by citizens. Framing the debate about responses to media violence as solely about censorship is not only inaccurate but damaging to the very values the First Amendment seeks to protect. Too often, the First Amendment is wheeled out as a cannon from which to launch preemptive strikes against anyone challenging the levels of media violence, regardless of whether government censorship is involved. When it is used in this way, the amendment inhibits debate and thus invades the very principle for which it stands. Such rhetorical uses also make it easier for Americans to disregard lessons from other countries in dealing with censorship and freedom of speech, on the grounds that those countries have never had protections comparable to the First Amendment.

THE WILL TO BAN
AND CENSOR

To these accumulated honours, the policy of Augustus soon added the
splendid as well as important dignities of supreme pontiff, and of censor. By
the former he acquired the management of the religion, and by the latter a
legal inspection over the manners and fortunes of the Roman people.

EDWARD GIBBON, *DECLINE AND FALL OF THE ROMAN EMPIRE*[7]

The subjects that rulers have wished to censor have usually been ones
they considered religiously or politically dangerous, not violent entertainment. Indeed, such entertainment has rarely been high on any
society's list of topics to be banned or kept from public view. It was in
ancient Rome that the office of censor was first instituted to scrutinize
what was published from the point of view of whether it was politically
or religiously offensive; and it was in Rome that the poet Juvenal
coined the phrase that epitomizes the most fundamental challenge to
censorship: *"Sed quis custodiet ipsos custodes?"* ("But who is to guard the
guards themselves?")[8] Yet it was in Rome, too, that the bloodiest
gladiatorial games were offered, precisely *as* politically and religiously
desirable and as superb entertainment fit for men, women, and children alike.

Once Rome came under Christian rule, not only the games but all "spectacles," including concerts and athletic events, were condemned as entertainments to be shunned by Christians, whether as spectators, producers, playwrights, musicians, or actors. What the Church Fathers rejected as pagan in such spectacles were religious offenses of two kinds: the idolatry of pagan gods such as Bacchus, under whose aegis many Roman plays, athletic events, and musical concerts were held; and the impiety in reviling and joking about religion and about the Christian God. Adding to the offensiveness of all spectacles, for these authorities, was not only cruelty but also, and more often mentioned, bawdiness, obscenity, and general immorality. From that day to this, many critics of mass entertainment have found the depiction of sexuality to be more offensive than the depiction of violence.

Consider how spectacles in France, a society ever passionate about the stage, were banned or censored for over a millennium. Throughout the Middle Ages and long afterward, actors there were excommunicated and denied the holy sacraments and Church burial; often they were deprived of civil rights and treated as outlaws. The Jansenists raged against all spectacles as irreligious. According to Pascal, "All the great 'divertissements' are dangerous for the Christian life, but among all those which the world has invented, none is more to fear than the theatre."[9] The Church's castigation of playwrights and actors persisted in France even during the great age of playwrights such as Corneille, Racine, and Molière, when the public was mad for theater and when actors and authors received royal subsidies and pensions. The effects of such condemnations were far-reaching. Corneille had to "clean up" his plays by eliminating all mention, even, of kisses; Racine renounced the drama under pressure from Jansenists and others; and Molière was permitted a religious burial only after King Louis XIV intervened.

By the late 1600s, the objections to the theater in France were no longer strictly theological, but concerned, also, its more general effects on spectators, actors, and the public at large. Just as "impiety" and "idolatry" had been and remained the criteria in the religious battles over the role of spectacles, so "utility" and "justice" were the central criteria in the secular debate. Though impiety or idolatry might still be invoked in more secular discussions, the fiercest controversies now had to do with the utility or disutility of spectacles. Do plays serve to improve or to harm audiences? Are there special risks to women and others thought vulnerable? What of plays that are neither especially useful nor harmful but simply useless—should they be regarded as harmless entertainments or as a waste of valuable time?

The debate over utility invoked, on one side, a crude view, drawing on Aristotle, of theater as providing a "purgation" of the passions and, on the other, claims that the passions aroused by plays led viewers to imitate the licentiousness and the cruelty they saw on the stage. Thus the redoubtable Bishop Bossuet argued, in 1694, that the stage excites harmful passions even as it provides useless entertainment.[10] In offending decency and stimulating imitation, it leads to sin; in drawing viewers from work, family, and religious activities, it wastes time; in allowing women to exhibit themselves on the stage, it promotes what is tantamount to prostitution.

Once the religious prohibition of all spectacles could be questioned, methods of censorship were institutionalized as an alternative to outlawing them across the board. Official censorship, which was introduced in France in 1701 as the responsibility of the police, became a means for controlling what could and could not be produced and shown to the public. Works, including plays, that were seen as critical of religion, of royalty, and of public mores were the first to be singled out for prohibition. Certain plays, such as Molière's *Tartuffe*, were seen by critics as an outrage to morality, religion, the family, heads of households, and just about every other value society cherished. Throughout the eighteenth century, *Tartuffe* remained in the foreground of the debate over the stage—a symbol of its depravity to some, evidence of its glory to others. Even Molière's adversaries were hard put to deny his genius; what was at issue was whether his plays served to inspire disrespect for religious and other authorities, whether this was useful or harmful to the society at large, and whether, even if harmful, it was not a price worth paying.

Several compromises were put forward to allow plays to be staged rather than prohibited altogether. The most restrictive drew on Bishop Bossuet's restrictions on staging plays in religious seminaries: they could be tolerated so long as they were staged rarely, were conducted entirely in Latin, concerned a pious topic, and had no women, either as actresses or as characters impersonated by men.[11] A second compromise was to ban certain plays in their entirety but allow others to be performed. Partial censorship—what later came to be known as "bowdlerizing," after Thomas Bowdler, who published expurgated versions of Shakespeare's plays—constituted a third compromise. And a fourth involved rewriting plays to "moralize" them and make them instruments of character formation. Thus the Abbé de Saint-Pierre suggested ways to make plays instruments of propriety, justice, and patriotism, and to rewrite the plays of Molière so as to maintain their greatness, yet perfect them from a moral point of view.[12] He recognized that this could pose a problem: How to carry out this reconstructive surgery without damaging the play?

In 1756, Charles Desprez de Boissy, a French lawyer, published a widely noted "Lettre sur les Spectacles," condemning all spectacles indiscriminately, whether they be Roman gladiatorial games or the plays of Molière and Racine.[13] With respect to plays, he proposed yet a fifth "compromise": that staging them be outlawed, but that the reading of them still be permitted. Even plays that could be read with profit became immoral when presented on the stage, he held, since they could arouse the passions and sway audiences to rely less on reason than on feeling; love scenes were especially dangerous, above all for women viewers, who "imbibe romanesque ideas from the theater and even disdain housework as a result."[14] He did not himself wish to go to the theater, even for purposes of doing research on the topic of his book, any more than he would go to a place in a river where one risked drowning. As for his opponents who claimed to enjoy the stage, their reaction only went to show how desensitized they had become to its risks.

Desprez de Boissy's praise for the little republic of Geneva, in which all theater was prohibited, helped to spark a debate about censorship and state controls that engaged the foremost minds of the Enlightenment. At the center of their disagreements, which cut across the millennial debate over the stage and resonate still today, was a larger conflict concerning entertainment more generally: its nature, its role, its potentially debilitating or ennobling effects on individuals and society, and the degree to which it might foster or stifle freedom, equality, and the opportunity for citizens to thrive.

GENEVA AND THE
BANNING OF
SPECTACLES

The drama is not tolerated at Geneva. It is not that they disapprove of the
theater in itself; but they fear, they say, the taste for adornment,
dissipation, and libertinism which the actors' troops disseminate among the
youth. However, would it not be possible to remedy this difficulty with
laws that are severe and well administered concerning the conduct of the
actors? In this way Geneva would have the theater and morals and would
enjoy the benefits of both.

JEAN LE ROND D'ALEMBERT, "GENEVA," ENCYCLOPEDIA, 1757¹⁵

M. d'Alembert's proposals provide the most agreeable and seductive picture
that could be offered to us, but [one that is] at the same time the most
dangerous advice that could be given to us. . . . One shudders at the very idea
of the horrors with which they adorn the French stage for the amusement of
the gentlest and most humane people on earth! No, I contend, and I bring in
witness the terror of my readers, that the massacres of the gladiators were not
so barbarous as these frightful plays. One saw blood flowing, it is true; but
one did not soil the imagination with crimes that cause nature to tremble.

JEAN-JACQUES ROUSSEAU,
LETTER TO M. D'ALEMBERT ON SPECTACLES, 1758¹⁶

Incest, parricide, murderous mothers, fathers forced to drink the blood
of their sons—these were the horrors recounted in Greek and later
tragedies that Rousseau felt soiled the imagination of spectators far

more than had the gladiatorial games in Rome. At what seemed to be the safe distance of over a millennium from the games and before the bloodletting of the French Revolution, the Roman spectacles had become an abstraction for thinkers such as Rousseau, Montesquieu, Locke, and Gibbon.[17] The injustice, the murderousness, and the paradox that such carnage could be found entertaining were seen as horrendous, to be sure, but definitely outgrown and thus without acute contemporary relevance for civilized society, unlike the many glories of Rome's laws and culture.

Playwright to the core that he was, Rousseau aimed to dramatize his comparison between the "spectacles" offered to Roman and French publics. In his riposte to his former colleague, the French mathematician and philosopher Jean d'Alembert, Rousseau attacked the French stage and the lifestyle of actors as corrupting and strongly endorsed the ban on plays in his native city of Geneva. In so doing, he aroused a storm of controversy, breaking for good not only with d'Alembert but with his close friend Denis Diderot, d'Alembert's co-editor of the great *Encyclopedia*, with Voltaire, France's greatest living playwright, and with the Enlightenment spirit for which they stood, advocating the freedom to publish and perform.[18]

Geneva, the only republic in existence at the time, was, for the *philosophes*, a model of peace, progress, and liberty, especially compared with France. It demonstrated that a city could be prosperous without oppressing its citizens or abandoning its republican simplicity and equality. Geneva's laws proscribed torture and allowed its citizens greater freedom to think, to assemble, and to write than did France. The one exception was the theater. Why should a city so enlightened in its views be more illiberal even than censor-ridden France and other nations by prohibiting the performance of all plays and the visits of companies of actors?

In his "Preliminary Discourse" to the *Encyclopedia*, d'Alembert had already defined the indispensable role that he thought theater occupied in society. He had set forth a "system of human knowledge" in which the three principal faculties of the understanding are memory, reason, and imagination; imagination gives rise to poetry, which in turn has three subdivisions, of which the dramatic is one, containing "tragedy, comedy, opera, and pastorals, etc."[19] Persecution of any of these expressions of the imagination was thus not only damaging to the works themselves and their authors but to all human understanding and knowledge.

Far preferable to banning spectacles, d'Alembert suggested in his article on Geneva, would be to discipline and guide the actors who enacted them before the public. In his defense of the theater, d'Alembert avoided any claim that all plays were necessarily useful. He made no mention of the purgative or cathartic qualities of tragedy for which Aristotle's name was often invoked—having in mind, perhaps, Voltaire's dismissal: "Never heard of that kind of medicine."[20] The most d'Alembert was prepared to say was that theater could improve the taste and delicacy of sentiment of citizens, to the profit of literature. He also left out all questions of the impiety of the stage, even as he omitted all discussion of its supposed corrupting influence, apart from that of the actors themselves, for which he proposed, as a cure, that laws be established regulating their conduct. By enacting such reforms, Geneva could counter the "barbarous prejudice against the actor's profession"; the city would then soon have a company of actors so worthy of esteem that they would become Europe's best. Geneva would thus become "the seat of decent pleasures, just as it is now the seat of philosophy and liberty." One would no longer be confronted by the dismaying spectacle of actors excommunicated by priests and treated with contempt by the middle classes; "and a little republic would have the glory of having reformed Europe on this point, which is perhaps more important than is thought."

In his response, Rousseau dismissed d'Alembert's proposed controls over the conduct of actors as unworkable. For Rousseau, far more than their conduct was at stake; it was the theater itself that was both a useless waste of time and harmful, in that it corrupted its audiences. The one exception occurred when the public was already corrupted, as Rousseau maintained was the case in Paris.[21] In that case, theater might act as a sort of antidote and at the very least help to occupy scoundrels and thus keep them from more sinister activities. But why should Geneva, less given to luxury and idleness, be saddled with a resident theater? And why should it be asked to lead the way, as d'Alembert suggested, in bringing about a change in the regulation of actors and in "moralizing" the theater? Rousseau was at pains to refute those who argued that theater could educate and purify the emotions. He cast a side glance at the Aristotelian view of *catharsis*:

> I hear it said that tragedy leads to pity through fear. So it does; but what is this pity? A fleeting and vain emotion which lasts no longer than the illusion which produced it; a vestige of natural sentiment soon stifled by the passions; a sterile pity which feeds on a few tears and which has never produced the slightest act of humanity.[22]

Theater, Rousseau held, can actually diminish the ability to feel pity by giving it a false outlet. As spectators, we find it easy to channel pity to the characters on stage and then to feel that we have "satisfied all the rights of humanity without having to give anything more of ourselves; whereas unfortunate people in person would require attention from us, relief, consolation, and work."[23] Women, moreover, can be swayed by the passions enacted on stage into imitation and abandonment of their womanly duties. As for women who make spectacles of themselves as actresses, they disgrace themselves by taking part in the deceit inherent in all acting and by exhibiting their lack of chastity; they corrupt, in turn, the male actors who work with them.[24]

When Rousseau's *Letter* was published, in October 1758, it caused an uproar. The Genevese clergy and citizens, while doubting that Geneva was the modern Sparta that he depicted, united behind him when it came to the stage, rendering the production of plays out of the question.[25] Voltaire was incensed. This "poet and actor," as Gibbon called him, felt supremely frustrated at having no major outlet for the writing that he cherished above all others.[26] Since the Paris stage was closed to him and Geneva outlawed all theater, he was reduced to putting on and acting in private theatricals near Lausanne and at his home, Les Délices, near the gates of Geneva. With his hopes for bringing theater to Geneva stymied, he conceived a new stratagem: at

Tournay, on French soil, only minutes from his estate at Les Délices, he constructed a minuscule theater, decorated in green and gold. It had room for only nine persons on stage, but it sufficed for festive productions of his own plays as well as others. People came from far and near to attend these performances. One can hear him cackling, as he relates his success in a letter: "I corrupt all the young in the pedantic city of Geneva. I create pleasures. The preachers rage; I crush them. Let it be thus for all the insolent priests and all the hypocrites."[27]

In 1759, d'Alembert published a reply to Rousseau's Letter.[28] Feigning incredulity at such severe arguments coming from one known as a playwright and devotee of the theater, he dismissed as outlandish Rousseau's notion that plays constitute a more barbarian entertainment than that of gladiatorial combat, disagreed with his castigation of entertainment in general, and defended the stage as providing opportunities for moral growth and insight. To Rousseau's claim that some plays do the opposite, d'Alembert pointed out that no one would wish to do away with the benefits provided for us by historians or preachers or books on ethics just because some of them are ineffectual or worse. Rousseau's berating all actresses for disgraceful conduct failed to make distinctions among them; and his "sortie against actresses has led to a more violent one still against other women." In denying them freedom and education, he argued, what was at stake is not only culture and human preferences but the most basic justice to one half of humanity.

Both sides in the controversy found vindication, of a sort, in the events of the French Revolution. Not until 1789 were French playwrights able to write for the stage without fear of provoking the anathema of the Church; nor were actors eligible, in principle, for citizenship or allowed to marry legally.[29] Censorship was briefly abolished, and the press and the theater liberated beyond what d'Alembert and Voltaire could have imagined; but before long the patriotic festivals "breathing a certain martial spirit" that Rousseau had recommended for his native Geneva took on brutal forms he could not have foreseen. The instigators of the bloody spectacles of the Terror knew how to take full advantage of the high-sounding arguments that each side in the earlier debate had used, about freedom and justice, about control and virtue and community, and always about societal usefulness or harm.

Bans and censorship, whether religious or political or both, are rarely directed primarily toward violence, nor limited to entertainment. Their proclaimed aim may be, as in Geneva, to protect a thriving citizenry, yet they always threaten freedom. By now, governments aiming to maintain such controls are fighting a losing battle to channel and dam up the free flow of communication that is made possible by the Internet and other innovative technologies. Yet a number of these governments remain committed to censoring what they view as dangerous or corrupting material from the world's media, on grounds that their societies cannot thrive without such protection. One example is Singapore.

SINGAPORE, ASIAN VALUES, AND THE INTERNET

Singapore today, like Geneva in the eighteenth century, is a thriving city-state whose greatest resource is an industrious, well-educated, civic-spirited citizenry. Like Geneva, too, Singapore has instituted bans, censorship, and other limitations on freedom of speech in the name of protecting citizens from corrupting influences, often seen as coming from abroad. According to a letter from Mrs. Ong-Chew Peck Wan, deputy director of the censorship section in the Ministry of Information and the Arts,

> In Singapore, censorship plays a role in creating a balance between maintaining a morally wholesome society and becoming an economically dynamic, socially cohesive, and culturally vibrant nation. It helps protect the young against undesirable influences and safeguards central values such as the sanctity of marriage, the importance of the family, respect for one's elders, filial piety, moral integrity, and respect for and tolerance towards different racial and religious groups. It helps

to keep Singapore a place where we want to bring up our children.[30]

The letter explains that publications "are vetted less stringently than films," but TV, with its greater reach and accessibility to children at home, "even more stringently than films," as are video games because of their accessibility and their appeal to the young.[31] Comic books with extreme violence such as "gouging out of the eyes, disembowelment (with guts spilling out), cannibalism, dismemberment" are also disallowed: since while they may be intended for adults, they are easily accessible to children.[32]

Just as Rousseau pointed to the risk of corrupting influences from Paris and its spectacles, so authorities in Singapore as in a number of Asian states warn of the dangers of Western cultural influences and in particular those of the United States. Such pronouncements are made more often by religious and political authorities in defense of their censorship of criticism and political debate than by citizen groups. But it would be too easy to dismiss all rejection of the influx of Western influences as politically motivated. Some of the material that Asian governments regard as offensive is likewise a cause for concern in many other countries, including our own. Internet sites for terrorism, criminal networks, bomb-making instructions, and violent pornography, for example, pose special problems for all societies, including those with strict protections for freedom of speech.

Authorities in Singapore, too, are finding that the screening process they have instituted is turning out to be increasingly permeable. In September 1996, the government instituted a licensing scheme for the Internet. But if the government blocks a particular home page, it can be renamed so as to constitute a new home page. And information copied from any home page can also be sent as ordinary E-mail to recipients in Singapore. According to a 1997 survey article on Singapore in the *Financial Times*, the Singapore Broadcasting Authority admits that the Internet cannot be controlled. One official is quoted as saying that "equipment installed to block access to pornographic and other 'undesirable' sites should only be seen as a 'symbolic gesture.'"[33]

Many societies that engage in far less official censorship are likewise finding that the advent of the Internet makes it virtually impossible to limit access to even the most extreme violent and pornographic material. Partly as a result, legal prohibitions are increasingly difficult to maintain in more traditional media as well. Why censor or enforce bans on films of materials that are easily available elsewhere? Consider, for example, Sweden's long-standing practice of censoring extreme violence in films and, more recently, videos—the one exception to its strict constitutional guarantee against censorship. Before films can be publicly shown, they must be examined by censors to approve them and to determine what age limits should be set for children.[34] The law has been increasingly challenged, however. Efforts to prevent public showings of films such as *Natural Born Killers* have failed, with the result that films that would have encountered censorship in the past no longer do. Only films containing highly explicit pornographic violence have been subject to court decisions in recent years.[35]

Technological change has also contributed to weakening even the most ruthless forms of censorship. With the advent of video-cameras, fax machines, satellite TV, and the Internet, no contemporary regime can count on the totalitarian controls once imposed by Stalin, Hitler, and Mao. There were no video recorders in the Nazi concentration camps or the Soviet gulags or the Chinese thought reform camps; nor could news of atrocities be instantly circulated worldwide by fax or E-mail. By now, modern technologies have supported freedom movements on every continent. Some states still manage to shut out new forms of communication, at least in part. North Korea, Libya, and Afghanistan still ban the Internet, and Vietnam imposes severe penalties for its unauthorized use.[36] But such controls cannot last, least of all in states wishing to take part in global communications for purposes of commercial, industrial, and scientific development. China, for example, hopes both to make use of modern technologies and also to keep out materials the state considers politically or culturally offensive. It is struggling to ban Internet sites that its government takes to be politically or otherwise offensive, such as those of *The Wall Street*

Journal, Playboy, human rights organizations, and reports from the Taiwanese government; but because the Internet was originally constructed for military purposes, so as to allow innumerable routes for information to travel, most experts believe it is only a matter of time before the official efforts will be circumvented.

For the time being, however, it remains extremely dangerous for individuals in repressive states to try to evade official control: permeable technological frontiers alone are not sufficient to safeguard human rights. Burma outlaws the unauthorized possession of networked computers and sets long jail sentences for those found to publish or distribute "unlawful literature." Iran's government attempts to keep out "unhealthy" sites and to channel Internet access through the Ministry of Posts and Telecommunications at high costs to consumers; it has also declared the possession of satellite dishes unlawful. But channeling Internet access hampers communication for businesses and universities, in addition to private individuals; and as disks and antennae for satellite reception are miniaturized, it will become increasingly difficult to force their removal from private homes. In Iran as in other societies with strict censorship, it is already possible to access banned Internet sites via telephone calls to correspondents in other countries.

Communications theorist Neil Postman suggests, in *Amusing Ourselves to Death,* that "the fight against censorship is a nineteenth-century issue which was largely won in the twentieth."[37] Across the globe, however, that battle is still raging. Thousands of writers and journalists languish in jails in more states than were even in existence a century ago; many others stay free only by exercising strict self-censorship with respect to writings that might threaten the powers that be. In the end, however, traditional forms of censorship will surely be defeated as the Internet and satellite television and other new media cross national and other boundaries more and more easily, reaching hundreds of millions of persons.

What will this greater permeability of barriers mean for journalists, writers, and all whose professions depend on the freedom to speak? Even as it will weaken the force of the traditional censorship dilemma for the long run, it will accentuate the problem of exercising responsibility in the face of unfettered transmissions of violent, obscene, conspiratorial, and criminal messages. As the old-style controls gradually erode and censorship becomes not only undesirable but impossible, it is more important than ever to ask where lines still can and rightfully should be drawn.

JOURNALISTS AND
MEDIA VIOLENCE

In the First Amendment the Founding Fathers gave the free press the protection it must have to fulfill its essential role in our democracy. The press was to serve the governed, not the governors. The Government's power to censor the press was abolished so that the press would remain forever free to censor the Government. The press was protected so that it could bare the secrets of government and protect the people. JUSTICE HUGO BLACK, 1970[38]

Because journalists have the strongest professional reasons to defend the First Amendment in opposing every form of censorship, it is especially tempting for them to use the amendment as a shield against any and all criticism of the media. In protecting the press against interference with its public service function, which requires full freedom to probe and to report honestly, journalists, editors, and publishers may then invoke the Amendment, as well, to resist debate about media violence and about their own responsibilities in this regard.

The understandable visceral reaction in newsrooms against any threat to press freedom can then lead to uncritical acceptance of the common rationales for avoiding debate about media violence: that the focus should be on genuine causes of societal violence such as guns, not on the media; that "violence" cannot even be defined; that nothing can change our society's inherent violence; or that it is too late to try to stem media violence, given all the news means for transmitting such material. As a result, even when they do not reject inquiries on media violence outright as incursions on free speech, many in the press avoid reporting on it in any but dismissive and superficial ways and deal gingerly with the press's commercial interests in sensationalizing violence.[39] We need a more careful examination of possible links between press revenues from advertisements for violent films and television programs and inadequate press coverage of the effects of TV violence. How influential are tie-ins between newspaper chains, magazines, and TV stations? What pressures arise, for magazines and newspapers, from the fact that advertisements of violent films and TV programs are sources of their daily revenue? To what degree is such advertising immune to criticism, in the same way that revenues from tobacco advertising long hindered reports on the effects of smoking?[40]

While commercial linkages can put a damper on the most probing examination of the media's vested interests in entertainment violence, a desire to attract attention, to reach larger audiences, to break through walls of indifference, whether for reasons of public service or commercial gain, can also lead journalists to sensationalize their own coverage. Even reporters who have no desire to titillate the public with images of violence often find themselves in an ambiguous position. It is not clear how they can cover gang shootings or events such as the Oklahoma City bombing in adequate detail without being accused of adding to the level of media violence? Nor is it easy to bring out the details of kidnappings or spousal murder so as to inform the public, without exploiting its fascination with the lurid details.

A combination of reportorial desensitization and a desire to break through the indifference of audiences is commonplace among television production staffs and field reporters. As a Swedish news program producer noted, in a study of changes among news staffs over the past decade, "One creates a shield. One makes oneself unfeeling, one has to, it doesn't work otherwise. We don't have the strength to engage ourselves in every image—if we did, we'd go crazy."[41] In turn, the more violent reporting often aims at getting through a corresponding numbing on the part of audiences. Thus a TV news reporter noted, in the same study, that "one has to show very strongly emotional images of victims of violence in order to arouse an indifferent public. A wall of indifference has to be overcome."

Such problems are perhaps sharpest for reporters, such as Bill Moyers, who are most dedicated to high standards in investigating media exploitation of violence. In 1995, Moyers aired a four-hour television series, *What Can We Do About Violence?* His team reported on the experiences of young people with violent crime, as both victims and perpetrators, interviewing many individuals and groups attempting to bring about change. Portrayals of brutality and suffering were surely inevitable in such a series; but the segment devoted to media violence provided especially shocking juxtapositions. Even as background voices explained how viewing violence stimulates an adrenaline rush and how violence combined with sex and humor is an especially effective attention-grabber, viewers could see images that left nothing to the imagination, an ear cut off with large gleaming scissors, bodies pierced and throats slit, smiling gunmen shooting police officers, and clips from slasher movies showing men's glee in raping and killing women.

These programs aired in prime time and, in reruns, on Sunday afternoons. When I wrote to ask Moyers whether he and his staff had debated the use of these images and considered providing parental advisories before the most gruesome sequences, he replied that they had indeed debated the problem before making their choice:

> While I abhor the media's use of gratuitous violence and violence for entertainment's sake, I did not see how we could talk about the pernicious impact of media violence without allowing the audience to see what we were talking about.
>
> Our series was aimed at people trying to do something about real violence and violence simulated in the media— parents, teachers, psychologists, counselors, ministers,

concerned citizens. You would be surprised at how many of
these people have not seen what their children have seen.
When they do they are no longer just concerned, they are
appalled. . . . Our purpose was not to shock but to show—to
show a serious audience of mature people the media content
that often gets discussed by them in a vacuum. I know that the
merits of this approach are arguable, and argue them my
colleagues and I most certainly did, but I decided as I did in
the interest of accuracy and honesty, trusting my audience to
understand why in this instance I would show them something
quite uncharacteristic of my work.[42]

Moyers aimed his program at adults "not to shock but to show."
His purpose was to help them understand and visualize the reality of
what most adults rarely see—the extremes of violence to which children are exposed to on a daily basis. Because reruns of his programs
aired during the daytime, however, many more viewers, of all ages,
were bound to see the programs than the category of adults at whom
he had aimed them. Perhaps Moyers and his colleagues had also had to
sift through so much violent imagery in preparing the show that they
became less alert to what might and might not shock less experienced
viewers. Using the medium of television to convey his messages
enhanced the impact that Moyers could have on his audience; but it
also generated the difficulties that he discussed with his staff as well as
the problems for viewers that he had not foreseen. All these points are
worth considering for journalists casting about for ways to address
issues of media violence and media responsibility.

Both the press and the public stand to gain if journalists scrutinize
their own role in media violence and explore the obstacles that stand
in the way of providing better coverage. Too often, journalists, like
members of many other professional groups, seek special immunity
from outside criticism and compartmentalize their own work as sepa-
rate from larger social issues. To the extent that they do so, they
contribute needlessly to the sense that the dilemma between free
speech and censorship is so insuperable that little can be done about

media violence, and so immutable that all forms of regulation and communal and individual self-protection threaten freedom of the press.

Although traditional barriers to the influx of violent materials may be crumbling, this does not mean that societies, communities, families, and individuals have no legitimate interests in protecting themselves against programs they take to be offensive or dangerous. Full-scale censorship of the media cannot work in today's world, but self-censorship is as potent as ever, underscoring the tensions that will always exist between freedom and self-protection—whether in the commercial, the political, or the artistic arena. These tensions cannot be adequately addressed so long as they are not freely and thoroughly debated in their own right, rather than being narrowly construed as forming an insurmountable dilemma: free speech versus censorship.

ADULT RIGHTS, CHILDREN'S NEEDS, AND THE LAW

Congress shall make no law respecting an establishment of religion, or prohibiting the free exercise thereof; or abridging the freedom of speech, or of the press; or the right of the people peaceably to assemble, and to petition the government for a redress of grievance.

AMENDMENT I, CONSTITUTION OF THE UNITED STATES, 1791

The State shall ensure the accessibility to children of information and material from a diversity of sources, and it shall encourage the mass media to disseminate information which is of social and cultural benefit to the child, and take steps to protect him or her from harmful materials.

UNITED NATIONS CONVENTION ON THE RIGHTS OF THE CHILD, 1989, ARTICLE 17[43]

Before the 1989 United Nations Convention on the Rights of the Child (CRC), neither the U.S. Bill of Rights, nor the French Declaration of the Rights of Man, nor any UN convention on human rights had made specific mention of the interests and needs, much less rights, of children. These earlier instruments had been assumed to cover basic children's rights, such as those to life or to freedom from torture, as being no different from the rights of adults.[44] But there had been no provision for interests and rights of children that might be different from those of adults; nor any mention of the special vulnerability of children and of their need for protection from practices such as commercial and sexual exploitation.

The CRC was, likewise, the first international rights document prepared in the age of the new media. The First Amendment's primary focus is on the citizen's freedom to speak out about matters of public concern and in particular to criticize the government, whether by means of the spoken or the written word. The Founding Fathers can hardly be expected to have foreseen the revolution we have now lived through, with respect to the media, from the original focus on the spoken and printed word to all forms of communication still protected as speech. The idea that the state should have any responsibility "to encourage the mass media to disseminate information which is of social and cultural benefit to children and to take steps to protect them from harmful materials" would therefore have struck most authors of earlier documents as beside the point if not preposterous. So would the CRC's claim in article 13 that "the child has the right to . . . obtain information, make ideas or information known, regardless of frontiers."[45]

Until the last decade, few legal scholars addressed the problems surrounding contemporary media violence. For many, the main focus remains on the traditional print media and on adult political speech in the United States.[46] While children still rarely figure in most free speech analyses, women now do, especially in feminist debates concerning pornography and censorship.[47] Entertainment violence is taken up primarily, in these contexts, with respect to sexual violence, and children are rarely at issue save as potential victims of sexual abuse. Questions such as whether violence can desensitize children or render some among them more aggressive are seldom discussed in such contexts. By contrast, the risks of exposing young children to pornography on television or the Internet has been extensively debated, most recently in connection with the Communications Decency Act, which was struck down as unconstitutional by the U.S. Supreme Court in June 1997.[48]

The 1990s have at last seen more attention by legal scholars to questions concerning the rights and interests of children in the context of today's media. Newton Minow, former chairman of the Federal Communications Commission, and Craig LaMay, in *Abandoned in the Wasteland: Children, Television, and the First Amendment*, hold that constitutional doctrine recognizes children as a special class of citizens who require special protections and suggest that the Amendment can be used "to serve and protect our children rather than as an excuse to exploit them."[49] The authors make a number of proposals that they claim would interfere in no way with the amendment and that would allow children access to nonexploitative programming: among their suggestions are a ban on commercials during programs for preschool children and fees levied on commercial broadcasters to pay for creating high-quality children's programming.

Law professor Cass Sunstein has likewise considered the role the new media play in the lives of children and levels of violence in the programming aimed at them. In *The Partial Constitution*, he argues, as do Minow and LaMay, that the purpose of the First Amendment was to encourage public debate, not to stifle it; and maintains that the Amendment has now come to safeguard speech "that has little or no connection with democratic aspirations and that produces serious social harm."[50] Sunstein holds that regulatory remedies for excessive advertising and exploitative programming on children's television might promote rather than undermine freedom of speech; but that "flexible solutions supplementing market arrangements should be presumed preferable to government command-and-control."[51]

In *Justice and Gender*, law professor Deborah Rhode addresses the debate concerning pornography and violence, suggesting that it ought to be possible to design legislation that would criminalize at least a subcategory of violent material. An example of such legislation "would be criminal prohibitions against sexually explicit visual portrayals of force or violence that lack redeeming literary, artistic, political, or scientific value."[52] Doing so would leave the spoken and the written word uncensored and would not be so phrased as to single out sexual violence against women. In *Speaking of Sex*, Rhode restates her support for such legislation; and even though she acknowledges that it would do little to remedy the prevalence of sexual violence or to promote gender equality, it might "somewhat reduce the availability of targeted material [at] relatively little cost to core First Amendment values. Films like 'Dorothy: Slave to Pain' or 'Pussy on a Stick' are not cornerstones of democratic discourse."[53]

Kevin Saunders, in *Violence as Obscenity: Limiting the Media's First Amendment Protection*, agrees with those who would ban visual portrayals of sexually violent material, but he does not see it as constituting the only category that should be banned: "Violence is at least as obscene as sex. If sexual images may go sufficiently beyond community standards for candor and offensiveness, and hence be unprotected, there is no reason why the same should not be true of violence."[54] Saunders highlights what many foreigners view as an odd imbalance in the United States between the regulation of sexual and violent materials; movie ratings, for instance, allow strongly violent films as family fare, so long as they do not contain even mild profanity or sexual content. He examines the scholarly literature and research concerning harm to children and to society from media violence and concludes that some more general form of censorship is needed.[55] Suggesting that the term *obscene* may derive from *ab scaena*, meaning "off stage" Saunders claims that it has often been interpreted as including violence that could not be shown on stage in ancient Greece and elsewhere, adding that obscenity law in the United States was not, until recent decades, limited to sex or excretion.

Saunders proposes that current First Amendment doctrine should be changed to allow for a degree of censorship of certain expressions of media violence. These expressions should, he suggests, be regarded as unprotected by the First Amendment, just as "sufficiently explicit and offensive sexual material" already is, according to the current test for obscenity, adopted in *Miller v. California*, which asks:

(a) whether "the average person, applying contemporary community standards" would find that the work, taken as a

whole, appeals to the prurient interest; (b) whether the work
depicts or describes, in a patently offensive way, sexual
conduct specifically defined by the applicable state law; and
(c) whether the work, taken as a whole, lacks serious literary,
artistic, political, or scientific value.[56]

To the degree that decisions such as *Miller* hold that only the
sexual can be obscene, Saunders suggests, "they are simply incorrect
and should be disavowed."[57] He considers drafting a new statute,
modeled on *Miller*, in which persons can be charged with promoting or
intending to promote material that constitutes "violent obscenity,"
using the *Miller* criteria but reworded so as to specify the appeal to a
"morbid or shameful interest in violence" that depicts or describes, in a
patently offensive manner, "actual or simulated: murder, manslaughter,
rape, mayhem, battery, or an attempt to commit any of the preceding
crimes."[58]

Judge Robert Bork proposes still more far-reaching censorship in
Slouching Towards Gomorrah. He regards the existing obscenity exception to the First Amendment as unworkably vague and would presum-
ably say the same about Saunders's proposal to treat violent material as
constituting an analogous exception. Instead, he argues for shifting
back from First Amendment doctrine of the past fifty years to permit
straight-out censorship, "starting with the obscene prose and pictures
available on the Internet, motion pictures that are mere rhapsodies to
violence, and the more degenerate lyrics of rap music."[59] Admitting
that it is not clear how effective efforts would be to censor the Internet
or digital films viewed at home, Bork claims that lyrics, motion pictures, television, and printed materials are still prime candidates for
censorship.[60] He does not discuss counterarguments against censorship, nor specify how his own version would overcome the technical
obstacles to enforcing the prohibitions he advocates. Rather, after
expressing fear of our coming to be "at the mercy of a combination of
technology and perversion," he simply declares: "It's enough to make
one a Luddite."[61]

For anyone wishing to counter the societal evils that Bork depicts, the Luddite response of rejecting technological change represents a bitter counsel of despair. It would do little to counter these evils directly and would no more stop the spread of modern media technologies than could the British Luddites who smashed textile machinery in the early 1800s. Ironically, to the extent that modern-day Luddites hope to gain a hearing, their messages will have to travel alongside the welter of images and messages they aim to combat, on the pathways of the very technologies, such as the Internet, that many among them reject.

In "Regulating Violence on Television," Judge Harry Edwards and Mitchell Berman are in agreement with Bork on one score: The First Amendment, as presently interpreted, cannot be made to provide the controls on media violence most commonly suggested.[62] But they reach the opposite conclusion to Bork's. The Amendment must be respected, they hold, not reinterpreted, even at stark societal costs. Writing with full and anguished awareness of the impact of media violence in American society, and basing their conclusions on an exhaustive survey of the legal and social science literature, they provide a persuasive analysis of the many different forms of controls of television violence that have been proposed in Congress and elsewhere.

According to Edwards and Berman, television violence is "entitled to the full protection of the rules the Supreme Court has crafted to govern content-based speech restrictions." Try as they might, they do not find that existing social science offers a basis "upon which one may determine with adequate certainty *which* violent programs cause harmful behavior."[63] They argue persuasively that it would not be possible to draw lines with respect to what is and isn't "graphic" or "excessive" violence that would not also exclude many news programs and artistic works that no one would wish to censor. The First Amendment cannot be stretched to tolerate such indeterminate censorship, the authors assert; accordingly they hold that any proposals, such as some of those made by Sunstein, Rhode, Saunders, and Bork, must be rejected to the extent that they involve government regulation of violent programming based on its *content*.[64]

Edwards and Berman conclude that most forms of censorship, whether they involve total banning or require special time zones free from violent materials, cannot be allowed under the First Amendment. At the same time, they argue that measures to label programs as containing violence or not could be lawful if designed to promote parenting; and that the V-chip and other methods to block incoming television programs do not single out particular kinds of content for government-ordained censorship or other control. In other words, parents or other consumers could block whatever type of content they desired, so long as the state did not dictate what form of programming should be prohibited.

Edwards ends with an eloquent personal postscript reaffirming both his support for free speech and his awareness of the risks that media violence poses for young people and society. He puts the moral dilemma felt by many Americans in personal terms:

> As a constitutional scholar, long-term law teacher, and fervent advocate of the First Amendment, I am not surprised by the conclusions that I have reached. But, as a father and step-father of four children, the husband of a trial judge in Washington, D.C., who works with the perpetrators and victims of juvenile violence every day, and an Afro-American who has watched the younger generation of his race slaughtered by the blight of violence and drugs in the inner-cities of America, I am disappointed that more regulation of violence is not possible. Like many parents of my vintage, I believe, in my gut, that there is no doubt that the trash our children see as "entertainment" adversely affects their future, either because they mimic what they see or become the potential victims in a society littered with immorality and too much callous disregard for human life. It is no answer for a parent like me to know that I can (and will) regulate the behavior of my children, because I know that there are so many other children in society who do not have the opportunity of the nurturing home that I provide. If I could play God, I would give content

to the notion of "gratuitous" violence, and then I would ban it from the earth. I am not God, however, so I do not know how to reach gratuitous violence without doing violence to our Constitution.[65]

We must take seriously the moral tension to which Edwards points, even as we should resist feeling immobilized by conjuring up a rigid dilemma between our duties to safeguard the interests of children and to uphold freedom of speech.[66] Such immobilization is needless on two grounds: first because censorship of the media is less and less feasible; second, because both producers and consumers have many ways to exercise control that are quite unrelated to censorship. The choices confronting consumers, producers, parents, citizens, and societies often clash and are sometimes incompatible in practice. Making one choice may well preclude others. But a strict dilemma between rejecting censorship and safeguarding the interests of children would be one with no escape, no way to transcend or to "go between its horns." As I turn, in Part Four, to the efforts made at home and abroad to overcome the broader moral dilemma, Edwards's postscript will stand as a reminder against any inclination to belittle or shunt aside either of its aspects.

PART FOUR

opportunities

*Suppose that the world's author put the case
to you before creation, saying: "I am going
to make a world not certain to be saved, a
world the perfection of which shall be
conditional merely, the condition being that
each several agent does its own 'level best.' I
offer you the chance to take part in such a
world. Its safety, you see, is unwarranted.
It is a real adventure, with real danger, yet
it may win through. It is a social scheme of
co-operative work genuinely to be done.
Will you join the procession? Will you
trust yourself and trust the other agents
sufficiently to face the risk?" [Or would
you say] that, rather than be part and
parcel of so fundamentally pluralistic and
irrational a universe, you preferred to
relapse into the slumber of nonentity from
which you had been momentarily aroused
by the tempter's voice?*

WILLIAM JAMES, PRAGMATISM[1]

OPENINGS FOR CHANGE

Early in our century, William James closed one of his last lectures by challenging his listeners to help shape an imperfect world. Would they want to take active, cooperative part in such a world or slumber safely on? Taking part would call for confronting hardship, wrongdoing, and violence with no assurance of success in bringing about some betterment of the human condition. James took for granted that most people would accept the challenge. Sheer interest coupled with a reluctance to give up prematurely would lead them to seize the opportunity to join in, no matter what the uncertainties and risks.

What are the opportunities for constructive response that acknowledge the risks both from media violence and from censorship? As we seek alternatives that address the perceived dilemma without sliding into passivity, we can learn from initiatives already under way here and abroad. Examples abound of steps that individuals, families, schools, communities, and governments can take without infringing free speech, much less emulating authoritarian societies. These steps range from initiatives at the personal level to societal policies and international agreements. They may involve policies presenting families with more choice of quality programs, organizing efforts by consumers, including PTAs and other parents' organizations, wide-ranging press inquiry, and collective action by screenwriters, actors, health professionals, and many others.

The 1990s have seen a sharp increase in the number of studies of media violence and of self-help literature for persons who want to break out of burdensome viewing habits.[2] During this period, many citizen campaigns have also been undertaken, along with consumer boycotts and negative publicity directed at the producers and commercial sponsors of violent programming. And numerous legislative proposals have been made for regulations concerning ratings, filtering devices, and "watershed hours" before which violent programming is controlled.

Increasingly, the most effective responses to the problems of media violence are those that make imaginative use of the media. New technologies such as browsers and filters make it possible for consumers to be selective and to shut out unwanted programming. Many research and advocacy organizations distribute videotapes and other audiovisual materials, and a number already have websites for purposes of exchanging views and providing information.[3] Just as those who produce and market media violence operate on a global scale, so consumers and concerned organizations now benefit from worldwide exchanges and collaboration.

To undertake collective responses today without enlisting the Internet, television, and other contemporary forms of communication would be as quixotic as to try to return to primitive bartering in commerce. It would be just as shortsighted to see either media technology or money as good or evil in its own right rather than as a means for bringing about good or evil results. Aristotle made a similar reply to those who, in his own time, criticized the newfangled recourse to *rhetoric*—the use of language in law, politics, and other arenas of discourse to affect the emotions of listeners and influence them for or against different courses of action:

> If it is argued that one who makes an unfair use of such faculty
> of speech may do a great deal of harm, this objection applies

equally to all good things except virtue, and above all to those things which are most useful, such as strength, health, wealth, generalship; for as these, rightly used, may be of the greatest benefit, so, wrongly used, they may do an equal amount of harm.[4]

This is not to say that some individuals cannot try to lead their lives without recourse to the new media, only that these media can be either rightly or wrongly used, for beneficial or harmful purposes. We need to consider, therefore, how best to exercise initiative, creativity, and self-reliance as media consumers and as participants in the production and distribution of programming; and how to forestall the premature or excessive or degrading exposure of children to exploitative screen programming. But although children, being most vulnerable, should be at the center of our concerns, all of us, at whatever age, have reason to guard against ways in which violent entertainment affects our prospects for growing in understanding of ourselves and others and thus in our ability to deal most effectively with violence.

CAVEAT EMPTOR

The on/off button remains the first and simplest defense against screen programming that viewers find offensive, exploitative, or simply a waste of time. Some go farther, preferring not to be on the receiving end of any screen images whatsoever. Among families with small children, a number forgo access to cable television because of its multiplicity of channels, some of which broadcast films and programs more violent than any permitted on network TV. Others block out certain channels; still others limit viewing to certain times of the day or go without it for days, weeks, or months. TV-Free America—an advocacy organization promoting viewer autonomy—suggests that those who wish to break their viewing habits and find alternative uses of their time start by cutting out all TV for one week.[5]

Many parents of young children are making a conscious choice to shift back to the custom of reading aloud that was once taken for granted in many households, sometimes also choosing from among the high-quality videos now available. Such approaches bypass not only the violence and other inappropriate material ubiquitous on many television channels but also commercials. Parents may also look for available high-quality programming and encourage children to use computers and the Internet as more active alternatives to TV viewing.

Technology is increasingly coming to the help of those who want to avoid ambush by images and messages they find objectionable. The V-chip—a tiny electronic chip embedded in television sets that allows viewers to shut out programs according to ratings of their contents— is only one in an expanding array of techniques that are coming on the market to enhance the ability of viewers to be selective. Originally developed in Vancouver, Canada, the V-chip (short for Vyou Control chip) has also been much debated in the United States. Beginning in 1992, Senator Paul Simon and Congressman Edward Markey held hearings that resulted in the Telecommunications Act of 1996.[6] The act requires that new television sets be equipped with V-chips, capable of reading ratings of "video programming that contains sexual, violent, or other indecent materials about which parents should be informed before it is displayed to their children," enabling parents to block programs, should they wish to do so.[7]

In 1996, the television industry announced that it would adopt age-based ratings for programs other than sports and news. In this scheme, TV-Y would specify programs appropriate for all children, TV-Y7 programs for older children, TV-G programs for general audiences, TV-PG programs for which parental guidance is suggested, TV-14 programs concerning which parents are strongly cautioned, and TV-MA programs only for a "mature audience." But because such labeling does nothing to inform viewers about whether the ratings for particular programs had to do with their violent, sexually suggestive, or other content, a number of groups voiced their opposition early on; and by 1997, new policies were being worked out with most networks and a number of cable companies for rating programs not only by viewer age groups but also by the nature of the contents.

As for the Internet, filtering software such as Cyber Patrol likewise makes it possible for viewers to block access to selected sites with violent or sexually explicit content or content falling into any other categories that they wish to block, promoting, for example, racist ideologies, gambling, or drug use. The increasing availability of such filtering mechanisms was cited by the U.S. Supreme Court in holding unconstitutional the Communications Decency Act, which outlawed sending or displaying "indecent" material on the Internet in a way that made it available to minors.[8] In so doing, the Court, in an opinion affirming the primacy of free speech even on the unfamiliar terrain of the Internet, rejected the notion that viewer self-protection constitutes censorship.

Can it be argued that viewer blocking, by means of technologies such as Cyber Patrol and the V-chip, nevertheless threatens free speech in that it opens the door for viewers to shut out unlimited categories of programming? Psychologist Edward Donnerstein holds that "V-chips invariably lead, unfortunately, to I-chips for indecency, S-chips for sex, R-chips for religion, and any chip in the alphabet you want."[9] But if producers or independent groups do the labeling rather than the state, there can be no problem when consumers choose to avail themselves of as many chips as they want. They have as much right to choose among the programs and channels entering their home on the screen as to be selective with respect to magazines and books. Whether people prefer to exclude violent or sexually explicit programs, or even what most regard as innocuous nature documentaries, the freedom to do so should be their prerogative. As for parents making choices concerning violence or sex for their young children, that is surely neither a violation of free speech nor in any other sense objectionable in today's media environment.

What about the claim that when a sufficient number of consumers make such choices, programs are taken off the air, thus depriving others of access to them? True, consumer choice ceaselessly affects the availability of programs in market economies such as ours. Yet access to violent programming is hardly shrinking. In a society with but a few channels or with state-controlled media outlets, such deprivation might indeed result. But in societies where cable channels and video archives are multiplying, variously offering materials catering to every taste, such claims of deprivation are increasingly unpersuasive.

All the arguments that are convincing when raised against government bans and censorship controls collapse when aimed at individuals exercising judgment in their own lives and for their own young children. If official censorship undercuts individual autonomy, viewer choice renders it stronger. This is one reason that in the United States, the debate about the rights of individuals and families to use screening devices has now largely been won, at least in principle. But in practice, powerful vested interests have a stake in reducing the opportunities for consumers to turn off and screen and select, in order to retain all possible access to the lucrative but volatile child market.

Even as media representatives have resisted all moves toward V-chips and other screening devices, they have nevertheless also used the advent of these technologies to argue against any further regulation of entertainment. Why, they ask, should the expanding arsenal of home screening and blocking choices not suffice? When the most powerful and immediate control button is already available to viewers and when more technological protections come on the market every month, there can be no need for the various regulations now being promoted, debated, and sometimes legislated. If most people, including the vast majority of parents, don't yet exercise adequate control, isn't that their problem, not society's?

Invoking the new technologies in this way buttresses the long-standing position taken by media representatives, that the responsibility for children's viewing must rest solely with parents. According to this argument, neither the state nor the entertainment industry should have to assume any obligation to protect viewers against harm from media violence. As Ted Herbert, president of the entertainment division of ABC put it, adults can handle TV programs like NBC's *Between Love and Hate*, which ends with a youth firing six bullets into his former lover, but children cannot: "This will sound like a paradox, but I don't believe we have to program the network and absolve parents of responsibility, as if it were our problem and not the parents' problem. Parents have to be responsible for what their kids watch."[10]

Such claims focus attention on the troubling failure on the part of many parents to shield their children from the desensitizing and brutalizing effects that large majorities of the public now ascribe to media violence. Most parents would surely guard their children, to the extent they could, from witnessing actual murders, rapes, and other mayhem; but even when they are at home and able to influence what their children see from babyhood on up, it still does not occur to many American parents to do the same with respect to the graphic violence their children observe on television. For parents tired from long work hours and with little time or energy to spare for children, television has seemed a made-to-order baby-sitter. Baby-sitters, in turn, rely heavily on TV to help entertain the children in their charge. Year by year, research has shown that the time parents spend with their children has been declining, from 30 hours a week twenty-five years ago to 17 hours a week in 1993.[11] The time that families currently do spend together, moreover, is often devoted, precisely, to watching television.

"Every day," Newton Minow and Craig LaMay caution in *Abandoned in the Wasteland*, "all across America, a parade of louts, losers, and con men whom most people would never allow in their homes enter anyway, through television. And every day, the strangers spend more time with America's children than teachers do, or even in many cases the parents themselves."[12] The authors cite Yale psychology professor Jerome Singer, who points out the oddity: "If you came home and found a strange man . . . teaching your kids to punch each other, or trying to sell them all kinds of products, you'd kick him right out of the house. But here you are; you come in and the TV is on, and you don't think twice about it."[13]

"Say what you will," a number of parents might well reply to the pediatricians, teachers, psychologists, and many others who are now urging them to do more to oversee the programs their children watch, "the fact is that television viewing at home is a great deal safer than the activities our youngsters might be drawn into outside the home: the brutality of kids on the block, the crimes in our streets, the drugs our children can be lured to peddle or consume. And many of us work long hours. We cannot always be at home, seeing to the education of our children, however dearly we would wish to be able to do so. Community resources are often lacking, and athletics and after-school programs have been cut back severely in many school districts. When work forces us to leave our children alone at home and to worry about their returning from school to an empty apartment or house, television can serve as a surrogate parent far safer than any other we have at our disposal." As for screening devices, not everyone can afford them, much less know how to program them satisfactorily.

Such arguments have a point. Even with the best will in the world, many parents are not in a position to follow the advice of experts and child advocates. Until recent years, the failure or inability of parents to exercise responsibility or of society to act has been reinforced by the lack of adequate information about the risks to children from violent TV. The same was once true with respect to lead paint, asbestos, and firecrackers. As soon as such risks are clearly established, however, the responsibility falls more squarely on both parents and society. Just as I suggested that the perceived dilemma discussed in Part Three, between free speech and censorship of media violence, is a false dilemma, so the dichotomy many see between state and parental responsibility for children's exposure to media violence is a false dichotomy. It no longer makes sense to claim either that it is solely up to parents to shield their children from the risks in question or that it is solely up to the state. True, parents do have a strong responsibility to offer such protection, now that the risks to children are more clearly spelled out and more widely known. But what of the many children who receive no such protection through no fault of their own? Toy manufacturers would not get far if they placed all responsibility for protecting children from dangerous toys on parents. And the drug industry is required to use childproof packaging for medicines children could accidentally ingest. In all such cases, any proposals that the whole burden of protecting children be put on parents would be quickly rejected.

Because most adults have only recently become aware of the risks associated with media violence—of brutalization, desensitization, fearfulness, and appetite for more violence—the means at their disposal to shield against these risks are still unfamiliar to many and intuitive to very few. But without that shielding, many children's opportunities for developing resilience and empathy will be undercut before they have a chance to understand what is at stake and to make informed choices for themselves. Just as exposure to violence exacerbates all the factors contributing to a failure to thrive, so efforts to limit violence in a child's life and to provide forceful, creative means of dealing with it enhance all the factors that promote resilience.

Some argue that the best way to make children stronger and more self-reliant is to expose them from the outset to accounts of extreme violence. The hope is that this exposure will show them life as it really is and give them the necessary callouses to prepare them for life. Media violence, according to this view, is to be welcomed, not feared. It might actually provide a kind of toughening that will stand children in good stead in the long run.[14] But this hope turns out to be just as insubstantial as the belief that media violence might provide a cathartic effect and allow viewers to live out their aggressive impulses vicariously. The four effects of media violence combine to make children less resilient, not more, in dealing with real-life hardships and risks of violence. It is true that promoting resilience, among children as among adults, involves schooling the emotions through stories, and that violence cannot and must not be eradicated from these accounts. Long before children are ready for the great tragic works, such as Homer's *Iliad* and Shakespeare's *King Lear,* they learn about perfidy and cruelty through folk tales, myths, gossip, and the daily news. What helps them understand the role of violence is not concealing its existence, but first and foremost keeping from overloading their circuits with violence meant as entertainment and associated with glamor and thrill. Only if their understanding is not prematurely thwarted will it be possible for them to come to the fuller, deeper perception of the role of violence and to experience both the terror and the pity that genuine *catharsis* brings—what W. J. Bate calls the "enlargement of the soul," rather than Augustine's "stabbing of the soul."

When many families cannot cope single-handedly, when profiteers target young people with entertainment violence as with tobacco and guns, it cannot be enough to say that there is no larger responsibility outside the home. "Buyer beware" has always been an indispensable motto for consumers but rarely a sufficient protection. Least of all should children be left to shoulder the burden of self-protection when all else fails. Increasingly, parents, teachers, and communities are joining forces in rethinking how they should respond to the risks children face.

MEDIA LITERACY

How can children learn to take a more active and self-protective part in evaluating what they see? For an example of such learning, consider a class of second-graders in Oregon that Peter Jennings introduced on ABC's evening news in March 1995. With the help of their teacher, these children had arranged to study the role that television violence played in their lives: now they were presenting their "Declaration of Independence from Violence" to the rest of the student body. Their assignment had been to watch half an hour of television at home for several days running and to count the incidents of violence in each one—kicking, shooting, bombarding, killing. To their amazement, they had found nearly one such incident a minute in the programs they watched. The media mayhem they had taken for granted as part of their daily lives was suddenly put in question. One girl acknowledged that "before, I didn't even know what violence was."

The children then discussed the role of media violence in their own lives and concluded that what they saw on TV did affect them. Together, they considered different types of responses, often also discussing these choices in their homes. In their "Declaration of Independence from Violence," they addressed not only their school but the county board of education and community service organizations. Some pledged to limit their intake of violent programming and to refuse to watch certain shows; others wrote letters to television stations; a few organized a boycott of the products advertised on the programs they considered most violent.

These children were learning the rudiments of critical judgment and experiencing the pleasure of thinking for themselves about the messages beamed at them by advertisers and programmers. They were beginning to draw distinctions with respect to types of violence and their effects and to consider what might lie in their power to do in response. Throughout, they were learning to make active use of the media, including having their own initiative beamed to millions via the Jennings broadcast.

In so doing, the second-graders were participating in what has come to be called "media literacy education."[15] The media literacy movement, begun in Australia in the 1980s, views all media as offering scope for participants to learn not to submit passively to whatever comes along, but instead to examine offerings critically while recognizing the financial stakes of programmers and sponsors, to make informed personal and group choices, and to balance their own TV intake with participation in other activities. The hope is that children who become able to take such an approach will be more self-reliant, more informed, and correspondingly less fearful and passive, when it comes to their use of modern media. And since few adults have acquired critical viewing skills, such education is important at all ages.

Maturing, learning how to understand and deal with violence, coping better with its presence on the screen as in the world, knowing its effects, and countering them to the extent possible involves exploring distinctions such as the following:

- between physical violence and psychological and other forms of violence
- between actual and threatened violence
- between direct and indirect violence

- between active violence and violence made possible by neglect or inaction
- between unwanted violence and, say, surgery, performed with consent
- between violence done to oneself and that done to others
- between seeing real violence and witnessing it on the screen
- between portrayals of "real" and fictional violence
- between violence conveyed as information and as entertainment
- between levels of violence in the media and in real life
- between oneself as viewer and as advertising or programming target
- between gratuitous portrayals of violence and others
- between violence glamorized or not

Learning to deal with violence involves sorting out such distinctions and categories and seeking to perceive when they overlap and interact and shade into one another. It is as inaccurate to view all these distinctions as utterly blurred as to imagine each category in a watertight compartment. Exploring these distinctions and their interactions is facilitated by talking them over with others and by seeing them illuminated, first in the simplest stories and pictures, later in literature and works of art.

Because the approach must be gradual and attuned to children's developmental stage, a film such as Steven Spielberg's *Schindler's List,* which offers searing insight into most of the distinctions listed above, is inappropriate for small children, who have not learned to make the necessary distinctions.[16] If they are exposed to such a film before they have learned to draw even rudimentary distinctions with respect to violence, they can respond with terror, numbing, sometimes even misplaced glee. As far as they are concerned, it is beside the point whether the horrors the film conveys are gratuitous or not, real or fictional, or meant as entertainment or not. They cannot tell the difference and should not be exposed to such material before they can do so. The film can be misunderstood, too, by those who would ordinarily be old enough to perceive such distinctions but whose capacity to respond to them has been thwarted or numbed, through personal experience, perhaps from violence in the home, or through overexposure to entertainment violence. The half-embarrassed, half-riotous laughter with which some high school audiences greeted the film troubled many: it was as if these students had lost their ability to make even the most basic distinctions.

A number of these distinctions are hard even for the most experienced media critics to pin down. Take the concept of "gratuitous" violence, violence not needed for purposes of the story being told but added for its shock or entertainment value. Some regard it as a characterization primarily in the eye of the beholder, while others insist that it can be clearly identified in particular films and television programs. Whatever the answer, there are borderline cases of violence where it is hard for anyone to be sure whether it is gratuitous or not. Works, such as Spielberg's *Schindler's List* show instances of extreme cruelty that are necessary to convey the horror and inhumanity of the work's subject, and are thus not gratuitous in their own right; yet that film also explores how gratuitous violence is inflicted, even enjoyed, by its perpetrators. The film is about gratuitous violence, then, without in any sense exploiting it or representing an instance of it; and it is emphatically not meant as entertainment violence. Perhaps this is part of what Spielberg meant in saying that he made the film "thinking that if it did entertain, then I would have failed. It was important to me not to set out to please. Because I always had."[17]

Long before callous or uncomprehending ways of responding become ingrained, children can learn, much as the second-graders in the Jennings program were learning, to play a greater part in sorting out the distinctions regarding violence and media violence and to consider how they wish to respond. They can learn to think for themselves and to become discriminating viewers and active participants, rather than passive consumers of the entertainment violence beamed at them daily. Such learning helps, in turn, with the larger goal of achieving resilience—the ability to bounce back, to resist and overcome adversity.

Just as "Buyer beware" is an indispensable motto in today's media environment but far from sufficient, so is a fuller understanding of the role of violence in public entertainment. Individuals, families, and schools can do a great deal; but unless they can join in broader endeavors devoted to enhancing collective resilience, the many admirable personal efforts now under way will not begin to suffice. When neither families nor schools, churches, and neighborhoods can cope alone, what is the larger social responsibility?

COLLECTIVE ACTION

Each child born is a new opportunity. Each family can make choices and decisions that strengthen children and strike a small blow against the social toxicity that surrounds us. Citizens can put their money and their votes behind programs and policies aimed at detoxifying the social environment: establishing smaller schools; drawing closer ties between children and the community; defusing violence; resisting nastiness; turning off the television; being strong for children; making adult relationships work as well as possible in the child's best interest.

JAMES GARBARINO, *RAISING CHILDREN IN A SOCIALLY TOXIC ENVIRONMENT*[18]

As the profitability and dissemination of entertainment violence grow, as information spreads about its effects, and as children are increasingly targeted, more broad-gauged and forceful collaborative efforts are being mounted in response. In earlier decades, the debate about media violence engaged fewer people. Representatives of the entertainment industry stood nearly united on one side, supported by many intellectuals and artists wary of all threats to creativity and free expression. To them, it seemed a simple matter to wave aside reports of studies showing harm from TV viewing, much as the tobacco industry long dismissed research pointing to harm from smoking. On the other side of the divide, groups of teachers, pediatricians, psychologists, and parents were warning against the effects on children of a steady diet of TV entertainment. At the same time, members of fundamentalist religious groups were working to eliminate particular books from school libraries or particular programs from television programming— focusing not on violence so much as on crude language, sexual content, and the disparagement of religious, patriotic, or family values. Many on this side of the divide dismissed as alarmist any concerns about censorship that their actions aroused.

During the 1990s, much larger efforts by citizen advocacy groups, churches, professional organizations, public officials, and media groups have been launched to address the problems posed by media violence. The original advocacy organizations are still vocal; but many in the public at large, wary of polarization and overheated rhetoric, are considering collaborative responses that can be respectful not only of creativity, free speech, and adult rights but also of the needs and rights of children and of communities.

Citizen groups such as the National PTA and the National Alliance for Nonviolent Programming have mounted campaigns, formed watchdog groups, and lobbied for more quality television and for renewed sensitivity to the needs of children. Magazines—among them *Ladies Home Journal* and *McCall's*—have highlighted problems of media violence and suggested avenues for activist response. In 1994, America's Roman Catholic bishops released an antiviolence message, denouncing the "culture of violence" they saw as pervading American society and as fostered in part by the media, and urging parishioners and others to "persuade and dialogue with the sponsors of these programs that they have a social responsibility to the wider community."[19] Many other religious and nondenominational groups have taken similar steps. Some have focused on media violence; others have proposed that families voluntarily limit all exposure to television. The American Family Association has published advertisements naming programs and sponsors responsible for programs they take to be especially offensive. They have variously proposed letter-writing campaigns to stations, networks, and sponsors; boycotts of the programs themselves as well as of the products of the sponsoring companies; cancellation of subscriptions to cable networks offering such programs; and a number of other measures.

Inevitably, the groups sponsoring these initiatives have widely differing agendas. The U.S. Catholic bishops, for example, include abortion among the practices targeted by their antiviolence campaign. Some feminists, many of whom would disagree with the bishops on this score, oppose all programs they see as demeaning to women, whether or not they are explicitly violent. Certain conservatives see media violence as only part of a wide variety of other programming that should be rejected as too vulgar, too focused on sexuality, or demeaning to religious traditions. Liberals who focus on media violence often do so in the context of other measures to combat societal violence, including gun control, antipoverty programs, health care reform, and greater societal attention to the needs of children generally. Law professor Kathleen Sullivan has quipped that it sometimes seems as if the only aspect of programming that both conservatives and liberals can agree to characterize as offensive is sexual violence.[20]

What of the claim sometimes voiced, that such conflicting agendas are bound to undercut one another and, in turn, limit the chances of reform? This does not in fact seem to be happening. It is natural that there should be disagreement about many aspects of media violence and about how it fits in with other societal problems. If controversy brings the topic into public debate more forcefully, this already represents progress. Disagreement would be harmful only to the extent that positions became so locked in as to inhibit careful examination of existing empirical documentation and formulating policy alternatives.

In addition, it is possible for persons espousing widely differing points of view to come together in opposing the forms of media violence that have been found to be most damaging to children. When Americans do join together to support a particular agenda—as in backing the reforms urged by MADD, Mothers Against Drunk Driving—they can break through the public's inertia and challenge the special pleading by vested interests to achieve significant changes in life patterns. Why should it not likewise be possible for members of different traditions, beliefs, and allegiances to come together to combat the relentless acculturation to violence to which our children are subjected long before the age of consent? Whether it be members of women's groups concerned about our high levels of domestic violence, children's advocates pointing to the ever rising rates of child abuse and child injuries, or those who speak for communities in which minorities and the poor live with amounts of violence that have been compared to those in combat zones—all have an interest in making common cause. All would benefit from a more coordinated joint effort to bring about a change in our cultural climate and to empower consumers to influence what is offered to them and to their children.

Another criticism is sometimes heard of civic efforts to combat media violence: that they are elitist and as such are bound to fail, given that they will never involve a large enough segment of the public to have an impact. Why should it matter, critics ask, what a minority of the most educated, savvy media users choose to do in their own lives and for their families? This criticism is misguided for three reasons. First of all, the membership of many of these groups, and certainly of all of them taken together, is as diverse as all America. Second, the success of past movements in bringing about greater public awareness and behavioral change shows that it does not take a majority of citizens to call attention to a national problem and bring about reform (including reform on the part of the entertainment industry in cutting back on the glamorization of alcohol and substance abuse).

Third, even if only a minority of Americans decided to make changes in their own viewing habits and those of their children, taking a stance against violent programming, this would already have a powerful effect on the desire of commercial sponsors to underwrite the most violent shows aimed at children and young people. In a study of the effects of viewer discretion warnings on television, media analyst James Hamilton found that such warnings reduced viewership among 2-to-11-year-olds by 14 percent.[21] As New York Times television critic Walter Goodman has said, "Those who live by consumer acceptance can be slain by consumer resistance."[22] The effects of such resistance are already beginning to be noticeable, as public pressures and new options for exercising consumer choice multiply.

These changes are greatly aided by professional organizations such as the American Medical Association, the American Academy of Pediatrics, and the American Psychological Association, which have been in the forefront of efforts to evaluate the role of media violence and to consider appropriate responses. They have followed up the research that they have sponsored by publicizing more forceful conclusions and clearer guidelines than have existed in the past. By contrast, earlier commissions and panels of experts were short on policy proposals. They tended, after careful research and documentation, to bring forth only the feeblest suggestions for dealing with the risks whose existence they so amply documented. The National Commission on the Causes and Prevention of Violence, appointed by President Lyndon B. Johnson in 1968, commissioned a report on the mass media and violence. It concluded, after a thorough review of existing evidence, that mass media portrayals of violence were probably one factor that "*must* be considered in attempts to explain the many forms of violence that mark American society today," and that television violence in particular had the greatest potential for short- and long-term effects on audiences.[23] Yet the report's primary recommendation was disappointingly mild: that the mass media create a publicly sponsored and supported "Center for Media Studies" to conduct further research about the matter.

Health care organizations have not only sponsored, and evaluated research, they have also taken the lead in urging members to advise the public of the risks associated with excessive television viewing and media violence. Just as physicians have belatedly come to see it as part of their responsibility to ask patients, as part of a regular checkup, about their smoking habits, so pediatricians are now urged to ask parents about their children's viewing habits and "TV diet." The American Academy of Pediatrics suggests that parents should limit their children's television viewing to no more than one or two hours a day and be on guard against programming with sexual or violent content inappropriate for younger viewers.[24]

Political leaders, members of Congress, and officials in government have also addressed questions of media violence more forcefully in the 1990s than before. During the 1996 presidential campaign, President Clinton and Senator Dole, however sharply they disagreed about the need for gun control in controlling societal violence, were as one in calling on the entertainment industry to consider the effects of its programming on children and young people. Senator Bill Bradley has suggested that viewers who are offended by particularly egregious programs should find out who the sponsors are, who sits on their boards of directors, and where they live; then "send a letter to the members of the board at their homes and ask whether they realize they are making huge profits from the brutal degradation of other human beings. Then send a copy to all their neighbors and friends."[25]

Is calling those who profit from such programs to accountability by writing to them at home an invasion of their privacy? Or an exercise of free speech to be respected as much as their own? As the controversies regarding media violence accelerate, we can expect many new forms of speaking out on the part of consumers, including, as in the Peter Jennings program cited above, by children themselves. Since they have most at stake in the debate, they should be given every opportunity to speak out as consumers and to address those responsible for the levels of media violence coming into their homes.

Promoting alternatives to violent programming is an important element in the campaign. In 1996, after much pressure from public service organizations and citizen groups, the Federal Communications Commission took a step toward improved programming for children by ruling that each television station should provide at least three hours a week of "quality educational television."[26] Three hours may not seem like much; and the programs the networks propose for filling such a slot are often anything but high quality. But as Peggy Charren, founder of Action for Children's Television, points out, most reforms, including those that once began to address problems of pollution, have to start somewhere. This ruling represents a change in the right direction: now it is up to consumers to petition for strengthening it and implementing it across the board.[27]

Within the entertainment industry, the increased pressure from consumers, public officials, and child advocates has brought more open discussion of what responsibility the industry should assume. Having fought ratings to go with V-chips, arguing that mandating ratings constituted censorship, television networks agreed to provide them beginning in 1997. Much creative programming is now available for anyone scanning all the channels; and the children's programming on public television is consistently nonviolent. The field is wide open for importing excellent programs produced in other countries.

Last but not least, the press has every opportunity to contribute to this discussion by providing better coverage of the many efforts to deal with the problems associated with media violence. It ought to be possible, when reporting on contributions to this debate by public interest groups, industry officials, officeholders, and others, to provide the type of analysis routinely offered with respect to other societal problems such as health care and crime. But journalists will not be at full liberty to do so unless they explore the financial and other pressures on them to exercise self-censorship regarding media responsibilities. Only then will they be able to engage in the unfettered reporting devoted to societywide problems in which their own profession has a major financial stake.

Another way in which the press can contribute to the debate involves giving voice to the individuals with most at stake in the outcome of the violence debate—the children who know violence in their daily lives, the parents and neighborhood groups who struggle against sometimes overwhelming odds, the organizations mobilizing to combat violence, and the pediatricians and social workers who work to help individuals overcome its consequences. In this way the press can penetrate the resistance that many in the public feel to thinking about the human dimension of the problems linked to violence. What is not yet common, however, is to report in this personalized way on media violence in its own right. It is urgent to provide more extensive coverage of the research now available and of the plight of the young, the poor, the disadvantaged, and the vulnerable, who have been found to be most easily affected by such violence.

NATIONAL
INITIATIVES

As we consider the many approaches to deal with the influx of media violence in programs and games marketed for young people, the question arises: How might an entire society mobilize in response? Some societies offer few opportunities in this regard; in others, religious or political authorities impose policies from on high. It may be instructive to look at the experience of two democracies that have encouraged a broad-based public debate about how best to respond: Canada and Norway.

Canada offers an example of a nationwide effort to incorporate a focus on media literacy into a broad-gauged campaign to counter the effects of media violence. Canada has the second-highest homicide rates among industrialized democracies, after the United States; and U.S. media violence filters across Canada's borders without cease. The debate about how to deal with what many in the public regarded as excessive levels of screen violence had foundered repeatedly in the past on the issue of free speech versus censorship; and it had been impeded by a quest for the "definitive" study of the effects of media violence and the difficulty of bringing together the broadcasters, the cable industry, the educational and medical communities, regulators, producers, advertisers, and other interested parties to seek a solution all could accept.[28]

Two events galvanized Canadians into action. In 1989, fourteen young women were shot to death at the École Polytechnique in Montreal. And a 13-year-old girl, Virginie Lariviere, whose sister had been raped and murdered, launched a national petition to ban all TV violence; by the time she presented it to the prime minister in 1992, more than 1.3 million signatures had been gathered.

The petition called for state regulation; but when the government took action, it chose instead to stress voluntary efforts on the part of media producers and consumers alike. It gave the Canadian Radio-television and Telecommunications Commission the mandate to engage every part of the society in considering the growing role of media violence in the lives of children and young people. Members of the commission engaged in wide-ranging discussions with private citizens old and young, with executives from the cable industry and from pay-TV and pay-per-view organizations, as well as representatives of Canada's Advertising Foundation, Teachers' Federation, Home and School and Parent-Teacher Federation, and other organizations. The commission also sponsored public colloquia and took part in meetings in the United States, Mexico, France, and other nations to explore common problems.[29]

In 1994, the Canadian broadcasting industry initiated pioneering field studies of the V-chip. The focus on this and other technological approaches to parental control represented only about 10 percent of the Canadian response to TV violence; by comparison, about 80 percent of the commission's effort was devoted to public education, including media literacy and the support of quality programming for children, and another 10 percent to establishing voluntary codes, agreed to by the Canadian entertainment industry, to ban excessive violence and to allow violence unsuited for children only after the "watershed hour" of nine P.M.[30]

The Canadians recognized that the V-chip empowers parents to protect their children only if they choose to do so; more is needed to provide consumers with the knowledge and understanding to use their new power wisely. In the United States, by contrast, the V-chip is often debated in isolation from issues of media literacy, high-quality TV for children, and industry self-restraint, and it has therefore often been vested with extravagant symbolic meaning in the larger conflicts over entertainment violence. For some, it has conjured up hopes of near-magical powers for parents to regain control over what their children watch; others have dismissed it as tilting at windmills, or decried its deceptive appeal as a magic bullet that could permit parents and society to continue ignoring the real needs of their children.

Canada's approach presents a model for other societies to study as they seek to respond to public concern and to facilitate debate about measures to deal with media violence. It is a model, too, for building consensus and exploring alternative policies without being sidetracked by simplistic rationales and false dilemmas. It shows how cooperative discussions can serve an educational function for media representatives as well as for the general public, and it illustrates the advantages of making partial improvements over doing nothing. It demonstrates the possibility of cutting back on the amount of violence reaching children and of making possible broader changes, once the societal burden of media violence is recognized and shouldered by all who play a role in its production.

Former CTRC chairman Keith Spicer describes this approach as "consensual and cooperative, not legalistic and coercive"—one that

> aims to keep program decision-making away from regulators
> and throw it back where it belongs, to thoughtful producers,
> script-writers, advertisers and distributors listening to more
> informed, better-equipped parents. . . . We believe that—as
> with pollution, drunk driving, and smoking—long-term public
> discussion can make obsessive violence directed at children
> socially unacceptable.[31]

The Norwegian government could draw on Canada's experience as it launched its own campaign, in 1993, "to combat violence in the visual media."[32] This campaign was part of an even broader effort to deal with every aspect of societal violence. While under Nazi occupation during World War II, Norway had experienced the most stringent censorship and attempts to impose every other form of totalitarian control. A vibrant resistance movement had blunted these controls to some extent; but Norwegians had come to know firsthand, as few other democratic societies, the evils under regimes exercising such controls.

Five decades after the war, a new sort of resistance was needed. By the 1990s, violent crime was on the rise in Norway. Its rates were still among the world's lowest, but that was no reason for complacency. Young males in particular were turning to violence more often, and increasing numbers of elderly people, children, and women were beginning to fear for their safety. The campaign to resist violence in the visual media was only part of a larger public effort to bring about a "safer, warmer, and more just society with a higher quality of life" for all citizens. The aim, the organizers declared, was not only to reduce violence but to increase Norway's traditionally high levels of resilience, empathy, and community cohesiveness. Since viewers cannot change or react directly to the violent situations on the screen, the organizers warned, they may develop an emotionally passive remoteness to what they subsequently experience in real life:

> If our capacity to react to injustice and violence is weakened,
> we will get a colder society. Thus the way may be paved for an
> even greater increase of violence as an expression of frustration
> and the need for self-assertion, and as a means of conflict
> resolution in the local community and the family.[33]

Among the aims of the campaign were to have the government work with citizen groups and the media to generate a "broad mobilization against violence in the media, to create awareness of the public's power and responsibility, to give priority to children and adolescents as a target group, [and] to place responsibility on those who disseminate media violence."[34] The Norwegians also aimed to disseminate greater knowledge of the visual media and to foster greater understanding of the visual language, to enable consumers to make more critical and conscious use of the media. Such a campaign would require consistent efforts in the schools, as well as strengthened adult education courses in media literacy.

The planners of the campaign knew that Norway could not, by itself, guard against programming originating abroad. Therefore, they initiated broader contacts with other Scandinavian countries, with the European Council, and with organizations worldwide to facilitate greater international collaboration in dealing with media violence. But while recognizing the problems posed by the multiplying channels available to the public and seeking to meet these challenges, the authors of the Norwegian plan also rejected the view of those who find any technological innovation problematic. We must not forget, they insisted, the "fantastic possibilities for increased communication, knowledge, insight and new forms of interaction that the audiovisual media are opening up."[35]

It was equally important, the Norwegians believed, not to blame the media for every outbreak of violence. The temptation to do so was strong when, in the fall of 1994, a case arose that was reminiscent of the killing of James Bulger in Liverpool the year before. A five-year-old girl was found dead near her house in a suburb of Trondheim after having been beaten unconscious by three playmates, then abandoned in the snow. The public was incensed and quick to blame media violence. The commercial television channel TV3 canceled the series *Mighty Morphin Power Rangers*, which was already under heavy criticism for its violence. A search of the homes of the boys who had beaten the girl revealed, however, no violent videotapes; nor did they appear to have watched violent programs on TV. A few weeks later, the Mighty Morphins returned to the screen. Instead of censorship, community efforts were mobilized to help friends and neighbors deal with the shock. Inquiries were made into ways in which the girl's death could have been avoided; and a broad-ranging debate took place in the press about the different causative factors that interact in precipitating any act of violence and about ways for families, communities, and society to counter each one.[36]

In both Canada and Norway, the campaigns have taken longer than at first expected and are still far from having achieved fully adequate responses to the problems of media violence. But both societies are better prepared to deal with these problems than they would have been had they not undertaken to learn about them and to discuss different approaches to them with all interested parties.

All who struggle to respond to the problem of media violence without leaping to overhasty conclusions—from the many groups active in the Canadian and Norwegian campaigns to the American second-graders who formulated their own "Declaration of Independence from Violence"—are concerned, at bottom, with achieving a measure of personal responsibility and independence that they see as endangered. In Part Two, I discussed the psychological and moral "failure to thrive" to which heavy exposure to media violence could contribute, through the effects of increased fear, desensitization, appetite for more violence, and aggression. For purposes of moving in the opposite direction, of protecting or enhancing a state of thriving, the choice must be to understand each of those effects in order to be able to reverse them; and to encourage, instead, greater resilience, empathy, self-control, and respect for self and others.

When the Canadians and Norwegians speak of their campaigns as involving "antiviolence," I take them to have in mind not only guarding against the four effects but also moving to reverse each one. In these ways, their stance goes beyond that of nonviolence to one of active resistance to violence. Much as being active in the antislavery movement of the last century involved more than not engaging in slavery oneself, so joining in an antiviolence movement has to go beyond opting for nonviolence in one's personal life. It calls for engaging in imaginative and forceful practices of nonviolent *resistance* to violence, including taking a stand toward entertainment violence. There is a world of opportunities for anyone choosing to take such a stand. Cultures are not frozen in stone. Violence is taught, promoted, glamorized; it can be unlearned, resisted, deglamorized. In the continuing contest between initiatives that can either enhance or debilitate human prospects, the words of Mohandas Gandhi still hold promise:

> We are constantly astonished at the amazing discoveries in the field of violence. But I maintain that far more undreamed of and seemingly impossible discoveries will be made in the field of nonviolence.[37]

NOTES

INTRODUCTION

1. Simone Weil, *The Iliad or the Poem of Force* (1942; Wallingford, Pa.: Pendle Hill, 1956), p. 1.

2. Bruce Knauft, "Reconsidering Violence in Simple Human Societies," *Current Anthropology*, vol. 28, no. 4, (August–October 1987), pp. 457–82, at 474. See also Robert B. Edgerton, *Sick Societies* (New York: Free Press, 1992), p. 474.

3. Knauft, "Reconsidering Violence," p. 475.

4. Knauft surveyed adult deaths over the period 1940–82, finding a rate of 3.07 homicides per annum, equivalent to 568 per 100,000 per annum. Ibid., pp. 462–63.

5. René Girard, *Violence and the Sacred*, tr. Patrick Gregory (Baltimore: Johns Hopkins University Press, 1977).

6. A poll by the Opinion Research Corporation of Princeton in January 1995 found that 82 percent of respondents believed that commercial television was too violent, especially for young children. See "Public Television and 'Elitism,'" editorial, *New York Times*, January 26, 1995, p. A16. See also Elizabeth Kolbert, "Despair of Popular Culture," *New York Times*, August 20, 1995, sec. 2, pp. 1 and 23; Daniel Cerone, "Most Say TV Violence Begets Real Violence," *Los Angeles Times*, December 13, 1993, p. 1.

7. Even though some of the most violent material is now being produced in cities such as Bombay and Hong Kong, as well as by international conglomerates, the United States still dominates the field. Such entertainment is often still attributed, in much of the world, to American producers alone. See Barbara

Crossette, "The Unreal Thing: Un-American Ugly Americans," *New York Times,* May 11, 1997, p. 1.

8. Howard Kurtz, "Murder Rates Drop, but Coverage Soars," *Boston Globe,* August 13, 1997, p. D8.

9. These are among the arguments I take up in a research paper: "TV Violence, Children, and the Press: Eight Rationales Inhibiting Public Policy Debates" (Discussion Paper D-16, April 1994, The Joan Shorenstein Barone Center). Rationales such as those I discuss serve a double function: They offer simplistic reasons for not entering into serious debate about a subject and thus provide rationalizations for ignoring or shielding ongoing practices from outside scrutiny and interference.

10. Michael Mann, director of the television shows *Crime Story* and *Miami Vice,* quoted in *New York Times,* October 22, 1993, p. C3. See also Jon Katz, *Virtuous Reality* (New York: Random House, 1997), p. 19; and Todd Gitlin, "Imagebusters: The Hollow Crusade Against TV Violence," *American Prospect,* Winter 1994, pp. 42–49.

11. For challenges based on diverging definitions, see, for example, John Leonard, *Smoke and Mirrors: Violence, Television, and Other American Cultures* (New York: New Press, 1997), p. 2. For an analysis of types of definitions of *violence,* see Sara Ruddick, "Violence and Non-violence," in Lawrence C. Becker and Charlotte B. Becker, eds., *Encyclopedia of Ethics* (New York: Garland Publishing, 1992), pp. 1273–76. For a distinction between *structural violence* and *behavioral violence,* see James Gilligan, *Violence: Our Deadly Epidemic and Its Causes* (New York: Grosset/Putnam, 1997), pp. 191–92. See also Virginia Held, "Violence, Terrorism, and Moral Inquiry," *Monist,* vol. 67 (October 1984), pp. 605–26.

12. For Friedrich Engels, the death of workers placed by society in such a position that they come to premature and unnatural ends "is as violent as if they had been stabbed or shot." Such a view of violence cannot be squared with narrower ones, such as that limiting violence to "the illegitimate or unauthorized use of force to effect decisions against the will or desire of others," or with yet vaster definitions such as that holding that "violence is present when human beings are being influenced so that their actual somatic and mental realizations are below their potential realizations." See Friedrich Engels, *The Condition of the Working Class in England,* tr. and ed. W. O. Henderson and W. H. Chaloner (Stanford, Calif.: Stanford University Press, 1958), p. 108. Robert Paul Wolff, "On Violence," *Journal of Philosophy,* vol. 66 (1969), pp. 601–16; and Johan Galtung, "Violence, Peace, and Peace Research," *Journal of Peace Research,* vol. 3 (1969), pp. 167–81.

13. John D. Searle, *Speech Acts* (Cambridge: Cambridge University Press, 1970), p. 55.

14. Such line-drawing with respect to media violence enters in when it comes to specific proposals for a system of rating violent programs or for limiting the types and degrees and amounts of violence in particular programs or at

specified times of day. At such times, agreement on definitions of what is to count as violence, gratuitous violence, and the like becomes crucial. Much can be learned, in this regard, by comparing the definitions and the procedures used in the rating systems already in place for motion pictures in America and abroad (see Parts Three and Four).

15. Oxford English Dictionary, "Violence."

16. Other distinctions include that between intentional harm and unintended or negligent actions resulting in such harm; between actions and omissions leading to harm; and between harm done only to persons and to nonhuman living beings and/or property.

17. H. Rap Brown, quoted at a 1967 press conference. For agreement on this score, see John Herbers, "Special Introduction," in Hugh Davis Graham and Ted Robert Gurr, eds., *The History of Violence in America: Historical and Comparative Perspectives*, a report submitted to the National Commission on the Causes and Prevention of Violence (New York: Frederick A. Praeger, 1969).

18. I ask respondents not to include countries at war or beset by civil war.

19. Lincoln Chen, Friederike Wittgenstein, and Elizabeth McKeon, "Human Security Crisis in Russia: A Failing Health Transition?" (Common Security Forum Discussion Paper, September 1996), p. 16. For global and regional comparisons of intentional injury deaths, see Christopher J. L. Murray and Alan Lopez, *The Global Burden of Disease* (Cambridge, Mass.: Harvard University Press, 1996), volume 1.

20. Fox Butterfield, "Serious Crime Has Declined For Fifth Year, F.B.I. Says," *New York Times*, October 5, 1997, p. A32.

21. See James Lynch, "Crime in International Perspective," in James Q. Wilson and Joan Petersilia, eds., *Crime* (San Francisco: Institute for Contemporary Studies Press, 1995), pp. 11–38, and Derek Bok, *State of the Nation* (Cambridge, Mass.: Harvard University Press, 1996), p. 219.

22. For proposals to deal with media violence in ways similar to existing policies on air and water pollution, see James T. Hamilton, *Channeling Violence: The Economic Market for Violent Television Programming* (Princeton: Princeton University Press, 1998).

23. Among such conferences are "World Summit on Television and Children," March 12–17, 1995, in Melbourne, Australia; "Children on the Electronic Superhighway," March 24–26, 1995, in Stockholm, Sweden; and the second "World Summit on Television and Children," March 8–13, 1998, in London.

PART I

1. Juvenal, *Satires*, X, line 79, tr. Gilbert Highet.

2. Martin Scorsese, quoted in "Violence in Our Culture," *Newsweek*, April 1, 1991, p. 48.

3. Nicolaus of Damascus, quoted in Athenaeus, *The Feast of the Philosophers* (*The Deipnosophists*), tr. Charles Burton Gulick (Cambridge, Mass.: Harvard Uni-

versity Press, Loeb Classical Library, 1927), vol. II, book IV, p. 199–201. Nicolaus, born around 64 B.C., adviser and court historian to King Herod the Great, reportedly wrote a universal history, now lost, in 144 books, covering the period from "earliest times" to the death of King Herod in 4 B.C. See also Keith Hopkins, "Murderous Games," in *Death and Renewal: Sociological Studies in Roman History*, vol. 2 (Cambridge: Cambridge University Press, 1993), pp. 1–30; and Christopher Jones, "Dinner Theater," in William J. Slater, ed., *Dining in a Classical Context* (Ann Arbor: University of Michigan Press, 1991), pp. 185–98.

4. The writer Petronius was characterized by Tacitus as the "arbiter of taste" who brought the "science of pleasure" to new heights at the court of Nero: "No imperial pastime or entertainment which lacked Petronius' approval could be regarded as either elegant or luxurious." Tacitus, *Annals*, xvi, 18ff, quoted in Petronius, *The Satyricon*, tr. William Arrowsmith (New York: Meridian, 1994), introduction, p. vi.

5. For accounts and discussions of the Roman practices, see Carlin A. Barton, *The Sorrows of the Ancient Romans: The Gladiator and the Monster* (Princeton: Princeton University Press, 1993); Paul Brantlinger, *Bread & Circuses: Theories of Mass Culture as Social Decay* (Ithaca, N.Y.: Cornell University Press, 1983); Kathleen M. Coleman, "*Contagion of the Throng*": Absorbing Violence in the Roman World (Dublin: Dublin University Press, 1996); Samuel Dill, *Roman Society in the Last Century of the Western Empire* (London: Macmillan, 1906); Hopkins, "Murderous Games," Richard Sennett, *Flesh and Stone* (New York: W. W. Norton, 1994), ch. 3; Paul Veyne, *Bread and Circuses*, tr. Brian Pearce (New York: Penguin Press, 1990); Georges Ville, *La Gladiature en Occident des origines à la mort de Domitien* (Rome: École Française de Rome, 1981); and Magnus Wistrand, *Entertainment and Violence in Ancient Rome* (Gothenburg, Sweden: University of Gothenburg, 1992).

6. Though some star gladiators survived for years or were given reprieves for life, the risks of dying were great for others. Gladiators had perhaps one chance in ten to be killed in one bout in the arena in the first century, and a much greater chance of death from then on. See Barton, *Sorrows of the Ancient Romans*, p. 13.

7. René Girard, *Violence and the Sacred*, tr. Patrick Gregory (Baltimore: Johns Hopkins University Press, 1977), pp. 1–9. Christian critics such as Tertullian and Prudentius saw the games as pagan human sacrifice; in *Contra Symmachum*, Prudentius also stressed the devouring aspect for spectators: "The pleasure fed on blood."

8. Dill, *Roman Society*, p. 54. See also Veyne, *Bread and Circuses*, part 4.

9. Coleman, "*Contagion of the Throng*," p. 5.

10. Ibid.

11. Martial, *Epigrams*, "De Spectaculis," 7, tr. Walter C. A. Ker (Cambridge, Mass.: Harvard University Press, Loeb Classical Library, 1968), p. 9.

12. See Kathleen M. Coleman, "Fatal Charades: Roman Executions Staged as Mythological Enactments," *Journal of Roman Studies*, vol. 83 (1990), pp. 44–73.

13. Tacitus, *Dialogue on Oratory*, vol. 29, tr. Peterson-Winterbottom (Cambridge, Mass.: Harvard University Press, Loeb Classical Library, 1970), p. 309.

14. Seneca could express himself more freely in letters to his friend Lucilius during the years before his death in A.D. 65 than during his years of service to the emperor Nero, first as his tutor, then as his counselor. Now he knew that he had already forfeited Nero's favor and that his end was near. Seneca's view of the games was conflicted; for though he spoke of the debilitating effects that attendance at the games could have on spectators, he went to the games himself and expressed admiration for the *virtus* or manly courage of the gladiators. They exemplified, to him, the readiness to die that he regarded as needed for anyone desiring true equilibrium and wisdom—above all in the mad Roman world under Nero, where lives could be snuffed out on the emperor's whim or an enemy's innuendo. The arena merely made explicit the fact of the danger of the world and the nobility of courage in the face of even mortal risk. The gladiator, therefore, could be seen as "a model of a wise man, who recognizes that his life can be taken at a moment's notice, and who submits to the discipline and the call of the master as of the deity." Cf. Seneca, *De Tranquilitate Animi*, 11.4–6. See, for a discussion of Seneca's politics and his equivocal role as Nero's adviser, Miriam T. Griffin, *Seneca: A Philosopher in Politics* (Oxford: Clarendon Press, 1976). Concerning Seneca's reliance on different forms of paradox, see Anna Lydia Motto, *Seneca Sourcebook: Guide to the Thought of Lucius Annaeus Seneca* (Amsterdam: Adolf M. Hakkert, 1970), preface.

15. Seneca, "On the Shortness of Life," in *Moral Essays*, tr. John W. Basore (Cambridge, Mass.: Harvard University Press, Loeb Classical Library, 1990), vol. 2, p. 331.

16. Seneca, *Letters to Lucilius* (Cambridge, Mass.: Harvard University Press, Loeb Classical Library, 1962), vol. 3, epistle 95, p. 79.

17. Ibid., vol. 2, epistle 88, p. 367.

18. Seneca's view of such loss of *humanitas* is preferable, I suggest, to references to "losing one's humanity" or to "becoming dehumanized." A number of thinkers, among them Immanuel Kant, Simone Weil, Hannah Arendt, and many contemporary philosophers and social scientists, speak of persons losing their humanity by participating in violence or deceit. Such language can too easily be stretched to legitimize denying full humanity to adversaries and oppressed persons, so as to come to think of them as subhuman, bestial, feral. The *humanitas* of which Seneca and other classical thinkers speak is less easily confused with humanity pure and simple: it is a rare good, a goal to strive for, an attitude to promote in children and young people. It is not clear, however, how Seneca's professed admiration for the courage of the gladiators, noted in note 14, squares with his view of *humanitas*. Why should gladiators give up their chance to grow in *humanitas* for the sake of fame and glory, all that Seneca regards as false glitter? Why should they consent, when given the choice, to participate in the

cruelty of the games? What nobility can there be in fighting to destroy others and to wipe out their own chances to grow in *humanitas*?

19. Seneca, *Letters to Lucilius*, vol. 1, epistle 7, p. 30.

20. See Louis Robert, *Les Gladiateurs dans l'Orient grec* (Amsterdam: Adolf M. Hakkert, 1971), for an account of the spread of the practice in Greece and the discussions it engendered there.

21. Ville, *La Gladiature en Occident*, p. 459.

22. Tertullian, *De Spectaculis*, XXV, tr. T. R. Glover (Cambridge, Mass.: Harvard University Press, 1966), p. 291.

23. Ibid., pp. 269–71.

24. Ibid., pp. 297–301. Brantlinger points out, in *Bread & Circuses*, pp. 86–87, that Gibbon discusses this "infernal description," by the "zealous African" in *The Decline and Fall of the Roman Empire*, vol. 1; and that Nietzsche derides the same passage in the *Genealogy of Morals*, XV.

25. Lisel Mueller, "Small Poem About the Hounds and the Hares," *Alive Together: New and Selected Poems* (Baton Rouge: Louisiana State University Press, 1996), p. 72.

26. Ville, *La Gladiature*, p. 471.

27. Hopkins, "Murderous Games," p. 5; Dill, *Roman Society*, p. 54. See also Simone Weil, "The Great Beast: Some Reflections on the Origins of Hitlerism," in *Collected Essays, 1934–1943* (Oxford: Oxford University Press, 1962), pp. 90–144.

28. Dan Barry, "Outcast Gladiators Find a Home: New York," *New York Times*, January 15, 1997, p. A1. See also Fox Butterfield, *All God's Children: The Bosquet Family and the American Tradition of Violence* (New York: A. A. Knopf, 1995), p. 10; and Nicolaus Mills, *The Triumph of Meanness* (Boston: Houghton Mifflin, 1997), pp. 43–44.

29. Sigmund Freud, *Civilization and Its Discontents*, in James Strachey, ed. and tr., *Standard Edition of the Works of Sigmund Freud*, vol. 21, p. 58.

30. Edward O. Wilson, *On Human Nature* (Cambridge, Mass.: Harvard University Press, 1978), pp. 105–6.

31. See, e.g., Hannah Arendt, *On Violence* (New York: Harcourt Press, 1969); Erich Fromm, *The Anatomy of Human Destructiveness* (New York: Holt, Rinehart and Winston, 1973); Girard, *Violence and the Sacred*; Konrad Lorenz, *On Aggression*, tr. Marjorie Kerr Wilson (New York: Harcourt, Brace, and World), ch. 14; Karl Menninger, "Innate Violence," in *The Crime of Punishment* (New York: Viking Press, 1968), pp. 157–89; Simone Weil, *The Iliad or the Poem of Force* (1942; Wallingford, Pa.: Pendle Hill, 1956).

32. American Academy of Pediatrics, "The Commercialization of Children's Television," *Pediatrics*, vol. 89, no. 2 (February 1992), pp. 343–44; and David Walsh, *Selling Out America's Children: How America Puts Profits Before Values— And What Parents Can Do* (Minneapolis: Fairview Press, 1995).

33. David Leonhardt and Kathleen Kerwin, "Hey, Kid. Buy This! The All-

Out Marketing Assault on Your Child's Heart, Mind, and Wallet," *Business Week,* June 30, 1997, pp. 62–67. See also James U. McNeal, *Kids as Customers: A Handbook of Marketing to Children* (New York: Lexington Books, 1992).

34. Elizabeth Kolbert, "Despair of Popular Culture," *New York Times,* August 20, 1995, sec. 2, pp. 1 and 23.

35. Madeline Levine refers to studies showing that 75 percent of parents set no such limits. *Viewing Violence* (New York: Doubleday, 1996), p. 49.

36. Friedrich Nietzsche, *Beyond Good and Evil: Prelude to a Philosophy of the Future* (1886), tr. Walter Kaufmann (New York: Vintage Press, 1966), pp. 158–59.

37. Friedrich Nietzsche, *The Genealogy of Morals,* XVI (1887), in Francis Golffing, tr., *The Birth of Tragedy* and *The Genealogy of Morals* (Garden City, N.Y.: Doubleday, 1956), p. 186.

38. Nietzsche, *Beyond Good and Evil,* pp. 158–59.

39. Wendy Lesser, *Pictures at an Execution* (Cambridge, Mass.: Harvard University Press, 1993), p. 261.

40. Wes Craven, quoted in Bernard Weinraub, "Long Live a Truly Good Scare," *New York Times,* June 12, 1997, pp. B1, B5. See also Walter Kendrick, *The Thrill of Fear: 250 Years of Scary Entertainment* (N.Y.: Grove Weidenfeld, 1991).

41. William James, notations to Alice James, 1896, quoted in R.W.B. Lewis, *The Jameses: A Family Narrative* (New York: Farrar, Straus, and Giroux, 1991), p. 555.

42. *New York Times,* October 30, 1995, p. C17; "Carmageddon," from description on cover.

43. Augustine, *Confessions* VI, tr. R. S. Pine-Coffin (New York: Penguin Books, 1961), pp. 122–23.

44. See Brantlinger, *Bread & Circuses,* pp. 78–80, for a discussion of this passage and its role in pamphlets and sermons warning against "the seductiveness of wine, women, song, games, gambling, plays, dancing, painting, novels." A more exact analogy, Brantlinger suggests, is with the "innumerable recent studies of the deleterious effects of televised violence on our own society of spectators."

45. James Alan Fox, quoted in N. R. Kleinfield, "Cruelty of Strangers: Arrests Evoke a Fearsome Trend," *New York Times,* June 23, 1996, p. 27.

46. Joyce Carol Oates, "I Had No Other Thrill or Happiness," *New York Review of Books,* March 24, 1994, pp. 52–59. See also Jack Katz, *Seductions of Crime: Moral and Sensual Attractions in Doing Evil* (New York: Basic Books, 1988); and Theodore Nadelson, "Attachment to Killing," *Journal of the American Academy of Psychoanalysis,* vol. 20, no. 1 (1972).

47. Oates, "I Had No Other Thrill," p. 52.

48. Dave Grossman, *On Killing* (Boston: Little Brown, 1995), ch. 5.

49. Psychologist Herbert Kelman has written of the Germans who engaged in genocidal murder and others as participating in "sanctioned massacres" in which they transgressed against ordinary rules of morality precisely because they were authorized to do so. Kelman speaks of authorization, routinization,

and dehumanization as the three factors that are interrelated and that lead to a weakening of moral restraints among perpetrators of genocide. Grossman, citing the Milgram experiments, speaks of authorizing, group absolution, and emotional distance as three factors in the conditioning used by the military. See also Nevitt Sanford et al., eds., *Sanctions for Evil* (San Francisco: Jossey-Bass, 1971).

50. William James, "The Moral Equivalent of War," (1910), in *Essays in Religion and Morality*, (Cambridge, Mass.: Harvard University Press, 1980), pp. 162–73, at 168. Katz, in *Seductions of Crime*, discusses the seductive qualities of crimes and their serving to transcend humiliation and rage. See also James Gilligan's discussion of the role of shame as a cause of violence in *Violence: Our Deadly Epidemic and Its Causes* (New York: G. P. Putnam's Sons, 1996).

51. William James, *The Varieties of Religious Experience*, speaking of drunkenness as "the great exciter of the Yes function in man," bringing "its votary from the chill periphery of things into the radiant core." As with all experiences of a cleavage between vision and action, those brought about by uncautious approaches to the radiant core may leave individuals with a consciousness of "inward hollowness" at the recognition that they cannot recapture or live up to the gleams of those ideals sensed near that radiant core—a hollowness that James sees as "one of the saddest feelings" besetting human beings. See James's *Principles of Psychology*, cited in Lewis, *The Jameses*, p. 440.

52. Grossman, *On Killing*, ch. 5.

53. Lawrence Jarvik, "Violence in Pursuit of Justice is No Vice," *Insight*, December 19, 1994, p. 21.

54. Joel Silver, quoted by Bernard Weinraub in "For This Movie Producer, Violence Pays," *New York Times*, June 14, 1992, p. H20.

55. John Woo, quoted in Bernard Weinraub, "A Specialist in Esthetics of Offbeat Violence," *New York Times*, June 30, 1997, p. B1.

56. In May 1994, a study of 867 Hollywood executives, directors, writers, and actors found that 59 percent thought TV and movie violence a problem, and nearly 9 out of 19 held that it contributed to the level of violence plaguing the nation. Kenneth T. Walsh, reporting on the survey conducted with the Center for Communication Policy at UCLA, in Monica Guttman, "A Kinder, Gentler Hollywood," *U.S. News and World Report*, May 9, 1994, pp. 39–46.

57. Committee on Communications, American Academy of Pediatrics, "Media Violence," *Pediatrics*, vol. 95 (June 1995), p. 949.

58. Martin Amis, "Blown Away," in Karl French, ed. *Screen Violence* (London: Bloomsbury, 1996), p. 18.

59. Ibid., p. 19.

60. Ibid.

61. Plato, *The Republic*, tr. Allan Bloom (New York: Basic Books, 1968), book 10, 605, p. 289.

62. For a discussion of Plato's views about poetry and contemporary views

of television, see Alexander Nehamas, "Plato and the Mass Media," *Monist*, vol. 71 (1988), pp. 214–34.

63. Iris Murdoch, *The Fire and the Sun: Why Plato Banished the Artists* (Oxford: Clarendon Press, 1978), p. 7.

64. Nicolas Boileau, *Art poétique*, chant 3, vers 1–4:

> *Il n'est pas de serpent ni de monstre odieux*
> *Qui, par l'art imité, ne puisse plaire aux yeux*
> *D'un pinceau délicat l'artifice agréable*
> *Du plus affreux objet fait un objet aimable*

65. Horace, *The Art of Poetry*, 182ff. in *The Satires and Epistles of Horace*, tr. Smith Palmer Bovie (Chicago: University of Chicago Press, 1959), pp. 278–79: "You are not to show on stage what ought to take place backstage."

66. Martin Verhoefen, quoted in *San Francisco Chronicle*, May 31, 1994, p. 23.

67. Aristotle, *Poetics*, chapter 4, 1448b, in Jonathan Barnes, ed., *The Complete Works of Aristotle* (Princeton, N.J.: Princeton University Press, 1984), vol. 2, p. 2318.

68. Aristotle, *Poetics*, books 14 and 6, 1453b, 1449b, tr. S. H. Butcher, in Walter Jackson Bate, *Criticism: the Major Texts* (New York: Harcourt, Brace, Jovanovich, 1970), pp. 27, 22.

69. Aristotle, *Poetics*, book 6, 1449b in *Complete Works*, vol. 2, p. 2320.

70. Bate, *Criticism*, p. 18. For discussions of Aristotle's views, see Amélie Rorty, "The Psychology of Aristotelian Tragedy," in Amélie O. Rorty, ed., *Aristotle's Poetics* (Princeton, N.J.: Princeton University Press, 1992), pp. 1–22, as well as the other essays in that volume.

71. A. A. Brill, *Basic Principles of Psycho-Analysis* (New York: Washington Square Press, 1960), p. 7.

72. The difference is even greater between the frequency of TV viewing and the infrequent attendance at the Greek tragedies that Aristotle thought capable of providing experiences of *catharsis*. As W. Hamilton Fyfe points out in the introduction to his translation of Aristotle's *Poetics*, "The Athenian could not go to the theatre every day. That would be emotional dysentery. He took his purge regularly twice a year." (Cambridge, Mass.: Harvard University Press, Loeb Classical Library, 1973), p. xiii.

73. Pliny, *Panegyric* 33, cited in Hopkins, "Murderous Games," p. 2.

74. For a discussion of the relevance of Aristotle's theory of *catharsis* to the effects of media violence, see the exchange of letters between Paul Goodman and Leonard Berkowitz in *Scientific American*, vol. 210, no. 6 (1964), p. 8.

75. Seymour Feshbach and Robert Singer, *Television and Aggression: An Experimental Study* (San Francisco: Jossey-Bass, 1971). Younger children were not included in the study; and the authors specifically excluded "realistic portrayal of bloody, sadistic, overly violent actions, not typically depicted on television."

76. Jib Fowles, *Why Viewers Watch: A Reappraisal of Television's Effects* (Newbury Park, Calif.: Sage Publications, 1992), p. 244.

77. Steven Messner, "Television Violence and Violent Crime: An Aggregate Analysis," *Social Problems*, vol. 39, no. 3 (1986); Linda Heath et al., "Effects of Media Violence on Children," *Archives of General Psychiatry*, vol. 46 (April 1989), pp. 376–79.

PART II

1. Leonard Eron, "The Impact of Television Violence," testimony on behalf of the American Psychological Association before the Senate Committee on Governmental Affairs, June 1992. *Congressional Record*, vol. 88, 1992, p. S8539.

2. Jib Fowles, *Why Viewers Watch: A Reappraisal of Television's Effects* (Newbury Park, Calif.: Sage Publications, 1992), pp. 229, 254.

3. Washington Irving, "Rip van Winkle," in *History, Tales, and Sketches* (1820; New York: Library of America, 1983), p. 770.

4. Introduction, PBS, "Does TV Kill?" *Frontline*, January 1995.

5. See Leonard D. Eron, "Relationship of TV Viewing Habits, and Aggressive Behavior in Children," *Journal of Abnormal and Social Psychology*, vol. 67 (1963), pp. 193–96; Eron, "Impact of Television Violence"; and Leonard D. Eron and L. Rowell Huesmann, "Television Violence and Aggressive Behavior," in Benjamin B. Lahey and Alan E. Kazdin, eds., *Advances in Clinical Child Psychology* (New York: Plenum Press, 1984), vol. 7, pp. 35–55.

6. PBS, "Does TV Kill?"

7. John P. Murray, "The Impact of Televised Violence," *Hofstra Law Review*, vol. 22 (1994), p. 811; Madeline Levine, *Viewing Violence* (New York: Doubleday, 1996), p. 6.

8. American Heart Association poster, 1992, reproduced in Gloria DeGaetano and Kathleen Bander, *Screen Smarts: A Family Guide to Media Literacy* (Boston: Houghton Miflin Company, 1996), p. 5.

9. See Neil Postman, *The Disappearance of Childhood* (New York: Vintage, 1982), pp. 96–97, for a discussion of the effects of children's early introduction to consumerism. See also Note 33, Part One.

10. Aldous Huxley, *Brave New World and Brave New World Revisited* (New York: Harper and Row, 1965), p. 44. See also Neil Postman, *Amusing Ourselves to Death: Public Discourse in the Age of Show Business* (New York: Penguin Books, 1984), Foreword and ch. 11.

11. Frederick Schauer, "Causation Theory and the Causes of Sexual Violence," *American Bar Foundation Research Journal* (Fall 1987), 737–70, at 753.

12. Committee on Communications, American Academy of Pediatrics, "Children, Adolescents, and Television," *Pediatrics*, vol. 96 (October 1995), p. 786.

13. Ibid., pp. 786–87. Although heavy television viewing is also correlated to children's poor academic performance and weak reading skills, the debate continues about whether television viewing specifically contributes to such effects in isolation from factors such as socioeconomic class, IQ, availability of books in the home, and parental education. See William H. Dietz and Victor

Strasburger, "Children, Adolescents, and Television," *Current Problems in Pediatrics,* vol. 21 (January 1991), pp. 10–11.

14. Victor Fuchs and D. Reklis, "The Status of American Children," *Science,*vol. 255 (1992), pp. 41–46. See also Martha Minow and Richard Waistbourd, "Societal Movements for Children," *Daedalus,* Winter 1993, pp. 1–30, at 5; and Sylvia A. Hewlett, *When the Bough Breaks: The Cost of Neglecting Our Children* (New York: Basic Books, 1991).

15. Marie Winn, *The Plug-In Drug* (New York: Viking Penguin, 1985), p. 148.

16. Dietz and Strasburger, "Children, Adolescents, and Television," pp. 8–31.

17. Ibid.; see also Aletha Huston et al., *Big World, Small Screen* (Lincoln, Neb.: University of Nebraska Press, 1992), p. 140; and Robert Kubey and Mihaly Czikszentmihalyi, *Television and the Quality of Life: How Viewing Shapes Everyday Experience* (Hillsdale, N.J.: Lawrence Erlbaum Associates, 1990), ch. 9.

18. Linda J. Sax and Alexander Astin, "The Development of 'Civic Virtue' among College Students," in John Gardner and Gretchen Van der Veer, *The Senior Year Experience: A Beginning, Not an End* (San Francisco: Jossey-Bass, forthcoming).

19. Milton Chen, *The Smart Parent's Guide to Kids' TV* (San Francisco: KQED Books, 1994), p. 94.

20. Elizabeth Thoman, "What Is Media Literacy?" (Los Angeles: Center for Media Literacy, 1995), p. 1.

21. See Jeffrey Cole, *The UCLA Television Monitoring Report* (Los Angeles: UCLA Center for Communications Policy, 1995); Dietz and Strasburger, "Children, Adolescents, and Television"; Edward Donnerstein, "Mass Media Violence: Thoughts on the Debate," *Hofstra Law Review,* vol. 22 (1994), pp. 828–32; James T. Hamilton, *Channeling Violence: The Economic Market for Violent Television Programming* (Princeton, N.J.: Princeton University Press, 1998). Levine, *Viewing Violence,* ch. 3; Myriam Miedzian, *Boys Will Be Boys* (New York: Doubleday, 1991), chs. 12–13. John P. Murray, "Media Violence and Youth," in Joy D. Osofsky, ed., *Children in a Violent Society* (New York: Guilford Press, 1997), pp. 72–96; National Television Violence Study: Scientific Papers 1994–1995 (Studio City, Calif.: Media-Scope, 1996); and Haejung Paik and George Comstock, "The Effects of Television Violence on Anti-Social Behavior: A Meta-Analysis," *Communication Research,* vol. 21, no. 4 (August 1994), pp. 516–46. See also the account and bibliography in Russell G. Geen, "Television and Aggression: Recent Developments in Research and Theory," in Dolf Zillman et al., eds., *Media, Children, and the Family: Social Scientific, Psychodynamic, and Clinical Perspectives* (Hillsdale, N.J.: Lawrence Erlbaum Associates, 1994), pp. 151–61.

22. See notes 75–77 in Part One.

23. American Psychological Association Commission on Youth and Violence, *Violence and Youth: Psychology's Response,* Washington, DC: The American Psychological Association, 1993.

24. For efforts to chart the different risk factors, see Mark L. Rosenberg and Mary Ann Fenley, *Violence in America: A Public Health Approach* (Oxford: Oxford University Press, 1991), pp. 24–33; and National Research Council, *Understanding and Preventing Violence* (Washington, D.C.: National Academy Press, 1995), p. 20.

25. Some have stressed three of these effects. The 1996 National Television Violence Study proposes three substantial risks from viewing television violence: "learning to behave violently, becoming more desensitized to the harmful consequences of violence, and becoming more fearful of being attacked." Levine sees most of the research to date as attempting to answer three questions: "Does media violence encourage children to act more aggressively? Does media violence cultivate attitudes that are excessively distorted, frightening, and pessimistic? Does media violence desensitize children to violence?" in *Viewing Violence*, pp. 16–17.

26. Ronald G. Slaby, "Combating Television Violence," *Chronicle of Higher Education*, vol. 40, no. 18 (January 5, 1994), pp. B1–2.

27. John Leonard, *Smoke and Mirrors: Violence, Television, and Other American Cultures* (New York: Free Press, 1997).

28. James Gilligan, *Violence: Our Deadly Epidemic and Its Causes* (New York: G. P. Putnam's Sons, 1996), p. 113.

29. William Shakespeare, *Macbeth*, III, 4. For commentary linking this passage to desensitization in media violence and in real life, see Martin Amis, "Blown Away," in Karl French, ed., *Screen Violence* (London: Bloomsbury, 1996), p. 13.

30. David Hamburg, *Today's Children* (New York: Times Books, 1992), p. 192.

31. Slaby, "Combating Television Violence," p. B1.

32. Estimates of the rates vary, from a thousand times higher for television characters to at least several times higher. See S. Robert Lichter and Daniel Amundson, "A Day of Television Violence, 1992–1994" (Washington, D.C.: Center for Media and Public Affairs, 1994); and David Walsh, *Selling Out America's Children: How America Puts Profits Before Values—And What Parents Can Do* (Minneapolis: Fairview Press, 1995), citing journalist Britt Robson, p. 66.

33. George Gerbner, "The Politics of Media Violence: Some Reflections," in Cees Hamelink and Olga Linne, eds., *Mass Communication Research: On Problems and Policies* (Norwood, N.J.: Ablex, 1993), p. 139.

34. George Gerbner et al., "The 'Mainstreaming' of America: Television Violence Profile" no. 11, *Journal of Communication*, 1980, vol. 30, no. 3, pp. 10–29. For discussion of research on the linkage between television violence and increased fear, some of which finds no such linkage, see Linda Heath et al., "Effects of Media Violence," *Archives of General Psychiatry*, vol. 46 (April 1989), p. 377. The authors conclude from the available research that "media violence frightens children and distorts their perception of the world." For a critical evaluation of Gerbner's research, see A. N. Doob and G. E. McDonald, "Television Viewing

and Fear of Victimization," *Journal of Personality and Social Psychology*, vol. 37 (1979), pp. 170–79.

35. Pierre Thomas, "The New Face of Murder in America," *Washington Post*, October 23, 1995, pp. 1, 4.

36. Joanne Cantor, "Confronting Children's Fright Responses to Mass Media," in Zillman et al., eds., *Media, Children, and the Family*, describes recent studies of children's responses to frightening programming at different ages.

37. Alison Bass, "Measuring TV News Toll on Children," *Boston Globe*, June 3, 1995, p. 1. See also Joanne Cantor and A. I. Nathanson, "Children's Fright Reactions to Television News," *Journal of Communication*, 1996, vol. 46, no. 4, pp. 139–152.

38. Paula S. Fass, *Kidnapped: Child Abduction in American History* (Oxford: Oxford University Press, 1997), p. 262.

39. Ibid., pp. 7–8.

40. James Garbarino, *Raising Children in a Socially Toxic Environment* (San Francisco: Jossey-Bass, 1995).

41. See, for testimony to this effect, Jerry Adler, "Kids Growing Up Scared," *Newsweek*, January 10, 1994, pp. 43–50.

42. Carnegie Corporation of New York, *A Matter of Time: Risk and Opportunity in the Non-School Hours* (New York: Carnegie Corporation, 1992), p. 30.

43. Fred M. Hechinger, quoting Zack, in "Saving Youth from Violence," *Carnegie Quarterly*, vol. 31 (Winter, 1994), p. 12.

44. Doris A. Graber, *Mass Media and American Politics* (Washington, D.C.: CQ Press, 1997), p. 213.

45. Cantor, "Confronting Children's Fright Responses to Mass Media," p. 139.

46. Martin E. P. Seligman, *The Optimistic Child* (New York: HarperCollins, 1996), pp. 6, 37–44. Seligman makes no mention of the effects of media violence on children or young people among the factors he lists as contributing causes to the rising rates of depression. It would clearly matter, however, to ascertain to what extent exposure to media violence interacts with the other factors. See also "Dialogues on the Brain," *Harvard Mahoney Neuroscience Letter* (Winter 1997), p. 5.

47. Michael D. Resnick et al., "Protecting Adolescents from Harm: Findings from the National Longitudinal Study of Adolescent Health," *Journal of the American Medical Association*, vol. 278 (September 10, 1997), p. 823.

48. Such trauma, long known to affect a proportion of veterans of wars, was classified as constituting a specific disorder only after the Vietnam War, when a number of those who saw combat returned plagued by such symptoms, often leading to impoverished human relations and inability to function in families or at work.

49. See Diane M. Zuckerman and Barry S. Zuckerman, "Television's Impact on Children," *Pediatrics*, vol. 75 (1985), pp. 233–40, at 234; and Betsy McAlister Groves et al., "Silent Victims: Children Who Witness Violence," *Journal of the American Medical Association*, vol. 269 (January 13, 1993), pp. 262–64.

50. The first criterion for PTSD listed by the American Psychiatric Association makes precisely the linkage between witnessing and experiencing that studies of children exposed to violence confirm: The person has experienced an event that is outside the range of usual human experience and that would be markedly distressing to almost anyone, e.g. a serious threat to one's life or physical integrity; serious threat or harm to one's children, spouse, or other close relatives or friends; sudden destruction of one's home or community; or seeing another person who has recently been or is being, seriously injured or killed as the result of an accident or physical violence. American Psychiatric Association, *Diagnostic and Statistical Manual of Mental Disorders*, 3rd ed. rev. (Washington, D.C.: American Psychiatric Association Press, 1987), p. 250. Reprinted in Jonathan Shay, *Achilles in Vietnam* (New York: Athenaeum, 1994), pp. 167–68.

51. It is known that trauma generates endorphins in a self-protective, numbing response, and that levels of serotonin in the brain are inversely correlated with aggressive behavior. Scientists are now studying the degree to which early abuse and neglect affect these levels and in turn predispose children to impulsive and potentially violent behavior. See Craig F. Ferris, "The Rage of Innocents," *Sciences*, March/April 1996, pp. 22–26; and Bruce Perry, "Incubated in Terror: Neurodevelopmental Factors in the 'Cycle of Violence'," in Osofsky, ed., *Children in a Violent Society*, pp. 124–49.

52. But unlike the concept of "thriving," which applies only to living beings, that of "resilience" (or "resiliency") is used also to describe fabrics and other materials that have the elasticity or buoyancy to recover their original form after being compressed or otherwise altered.

53. Roberta Apfel and Bennett Simon, "Psychosocial Interventions for Children of War: The Value of a Model of Resiliency," *Medicine and Global Survival*, vol. 2 (1996), p. A2.

54. Ibid.

55. Penelope Leach, *Children First* (New York: Alfred A. Knopf, 1994), p. 152.

56. Ibid.

57. Max Frankel, "The Murder Broadcasting System," *New York Times Magazine*, Dec. 17, 1995, p. 12.

58. E. B. Foa and M. J. Kozak, "Emotional Processing of Fear: Exposure to Corrective Information," *Psychological Bulletin*, vol. 99 (1986), pp. 20–35.

59. Slaby, "Combating Television Violence," p. B1.

60. Huston et al., *Big World, Small Screen*, p. 59.

61. Heath et al., "Effects of Media Violence," p. 377.

62. Mencius, tr. D. C. Lau (New York: Penguin Books, 1976), book I, part A, 6, pp. 82–83.; Immanuel Kant, *The Metaphysics of Morals* (1793) in Mary Gregor, ed., Immanuel Kant, *Practical Philosophy* (Cambridge: Cambridge University Press, 1996), p. 528.

63. Jerome Kagan, *Three Pleasant Ideas* (Cambridge, Mass.: Harvard Univer-

sity Press, 1998), ch. 3. See also Daniel Goleman, *Emotional Intelligence* (New York: Bantam Books, 1995), ch. 7; and Stanley I. Greenspan with Beryl L. Benderly, *The Growth of the Mind and the Endangered Origins of Intelligence* (Reading, Mass.: Addison-Wesley, 1997).

64. John Stuart Mill, *Utilitarianism*, (Indianapolis: Hackett Publishing Co., 1979), p. 10.

65. I use the term, not to denote some particular view of morality or some one moral tradition, but rather to stand for the development of basic psychological and ethical functioning stressed in all traditions.

66. T. Berry Brazelton, *Touchpoints: The Essential Reference. Your Child's Emotional and Behavioral Development* (Reading, Mass.: Addison-Wesley, 1992), p. 286.

67. Ibid.

68. Zuckerman and Zuckerman, "Television's Impact on Children."

69. D. Linz, E. Donnerstein, and S. Penrod, "Sexual Violence in the Mass Media: Social Psychological Implications," in P. Shaver and C. Hendrick, eds., *Review of Personality and Social Psychology* (Newbury Park, Calif.: Sage Publications, 1987), vol. 7, pp. 95–122.

70. Edward Donnerstein, Ronald G. Slaby, and Leonard D. Eron, "The Mass Media and Youth Aggression," in Leonard D. Eron et al., *Reason to Hope: A Psychosocial Perspective on Violence and Youth* (Washington, D.C.: American Psychological Association, 1994), p. 237.

71. Times Mirror Center for the People and the Press, "TV Violence: More Objectionable in Entertainment than in Newscasts," (Washington, D.C. (March 1993), p. 1.

72. Betsy Sherman, *Boston Globe*, "The Violence Factor: The Case for Hope and Freedom," December 15, 1995, p. B34.

73. Pauline Kael, "Killing Time," *New Yorker* (1974), in French, ed., *Screen Violence*, pp. 177–78.

74. Sarah Kerr, "Rain Man," *New York Review of Books*, April 6, 1995, pp. 22–25.

75. David Denby, "Annals of Popular Culture: Buried Alive," *New Yorker*, July 15, 1996, p. 48.

76. Rabindranath Tagore, "A Poet's School," in *Rabindranath Tagore: Pioneer in Education, Essays and Exchanges between Rabindranath Tagore and L.K. Elmhirst* (London: John Murray, 1961), p. 64.

77. David Finkel, "The Choices of Aaron Wolf," *Washington Post Magazine*, October 22, 1995, p. 12.

78. James U. McNeal, *Kids as Customers: A Handbook of Marketing to Children* (New York: Lexington Books, 1992), p. 249.

79. Aristotle, *Nicomachean Ethics*, tr. Terence Irwin (Indianapolis: Hackett Publishing Company, 1985), book 2, ch. 3, 1104b 10–13. For a discussion of Aristotle's views, see M. F. Burnyeat, "Aristotle on Learning to Be Good," in Amélie Oksenberg Rorty, ed., *Essays on Aristotle's Ethics* (Berkeley, Calif.: University of California Press, 1985), pp. 69–92.

80. Marie Winn, *The Plug-In Drug* (New York: Viking Penguin, 1985); Marie Winn, *Unplugging the Plug-In Drug* (New York: Viking Penguin, 1987); Jerry Mander, *Four Arguments for the Elimination of Television* (New York: William Morrow, 1978).

81. Daniel Goleman, "Brain Images of Addiction Show Its Neural Basis," *New York Times*, August 13, 1996, p. C1.

82. Håkan Jonsson, psychologist at the Backgården Center in Hedemora, Sweden, quoted in Jan Christoffersson et al., *Argument i repris* (Stockholm: Våldsskildringsrådet, 1997), p. 123. See also discussion of "stimulus addiction" in DeGaetano and Bander, *Screen Smarts*, pp. 56–59.

83. See, for example, Gil Bailie, *Violence Unveiled: Humanity at the Crossroads* (New York: Crossroad, 1995), p. 90. By contrast, sociologist Todd Gitlin, in "Imagebusters: The Hollow Crusade Against TV Violence" (*American Prospect*, Winter 1994, p. 45), estimates that an exceedingly high estimate of the deaths resulting from copycat crimes might be one hundred per year that would not otherwise have taken place: "These would amount to 0.28 percent of the total of 36,000 murders, accidents, and suicides committed by gunshot in the United States in 1992."

84. Ken Auletta, "The Electronic Parent," *New Yorker*, November 8, 1993, p. 74.

85. Michael Shnayerson, "Natural Born Opponents," *Vanity Fair*, July 1996, pp. 98–105, 141–44.

86. John Grisham, "Natural Bred Killers," in French, ed., *Screen Violence*, pp. 226–39, excerpted from *Oxford American*, Spring 1996.

87. Ibid., p. 235.

88. Oliver Stone, "Don't Sue the Messenger," in French, ed., *Screen Violence*, p. 237.

89. American Psychological Association, *Violence and Youth*, p. 34.

90. Edward Donnerstein et al., *The Question of Pornography: Research Findings and Policy Implications* (New York: Free Press, 1987), p. 118.

91. Paik and Comstock, in "Effects of Television Violence on Antisocial Behavior," identify fifteen types of situations for which research data most clearly support the conclusion that violent programs have an effect on behavior. See another list of fifteen factors in Edward Donnerstein and Daniel Linz, "The Media," in James Q. Wilson and Joan Petersilia, eds., *Crime* (San Francisco: Institute for Contemporary Studies Press, 1995), pp. 244–45.

92. Elizabeth Kolbert, "Despair of Popular Culture," *New York Times*, August 20, 1995, sec. 2, pp. 1, 23.

93. Edward Donnerstein suggests that correlational data indicate that early childhood viewing of mass media violence contributes 5 to 10 percent to adult aggressive behavior, in "Mass Media Violence: Thoughts on the Debate," *Hofstra Law Review*, vol. 22 (1994), p. 829. George Gerbner puts the figure at "at most five percent," in "The Hidden Side of Television Violence," in George Gerbner et al.,

Invisible Crises (Westview Press, 1996), p. 27. Karl Erik Rosengren, reporting on a 20-year study of Swedish school children in "Stor Fara med TV-våld," *Dagens Nyheter,* January 30, 1995, p. 5, holds that 10–20 percent of aggression in schools and neighborhoods can be "explained as direct or indirect effects of TV violence." For a view holding that such effects are slight or non-existent, see Jonathan Freedman, "Television Violence and Aggression: A Rejoinder," *Psychological Bulletin,* vol. 100, 1986, pp. 372–78.

94. Brandon S. Centerwall, "Television and Violent Crime, *Public Interest,* Spring 1993, pp. 63–64. Unlike those who have studied media violence in particular or examined amounts of viewing by different groups, Centerwall's research concerns the mere presence of television in communities.

95. Brandon S. Centerwall, "Exposure to Television as a Risk Factor for Violence," *American Journal of Epidemiology,* vol. 4 (1989), pp. 643–52.

96. See, for example, Kevin W. Saunders, *Violence as Obscenity: Limiting the Media's First Amendment Protection* (Durham, N.C.: Duke University Press, 1996), pp. 35–37; and Franklin E. Zimring and Gordon Hawkins, *Crime Is Not the Problem: Lethal Violence in America* (New York: Oxford University Press, 1997), pp. 132–33; 237–43. Zimring and Hawkins, focusing strictly on lethal violence, speculate that because time spent by large numbers of people with the media is time not spent by the most violent persons committing murder, the media may actually prevent thousands of acts of lethal violence a year (p. 128).

97. Schauer, "Causation Theory and the Causes of Sexual Violence," p. 753.

98. Jean-Claude Chesnais, "The History of Violence: Homicide and Suicide Through the Ages," *International Social Science Journal,* May 1992, pp. 217–34.

99. William H. Foege, Mark L. Rosenberg, and James A. Mercy, "Public Health and Violence Prevention," *Current Issues in Public Health,* vol. 1 (1995), pp. 2–9, at 3.

100. *Child Maltreatment 1994: Reports from the States to the National Center on Child Abuse and Neglect* (Washington, D. C.: U.S. Department of Health and Human Services, 1996).

101. Foege et al., "Public Health," p. 3; C. Everett Koop and G. D. Lundberg, "Violence in America: a Public Health Emergency: Time to Bite the Bullet Back," *Journal of the American Medical Association,* vol. 271 (1992), pp. 3075–76; Donna Shalala, "Addressing the Crisis of Violence," *Health Affairs,* vol. 12, no. 4 (Winter 1993), pp. 30–33. See also Garbarino, *Raising Children in a Socially Toxic Environment.*

102. Analogies with "epidemics" and "toxic social environments" should not tempt investigators to "medicalize" violence to the point of abstracting from personal responsibility. Being felled by gunshot and by cholera cannot be equated from a moral point of view any more than from a law enforcement point of view. See Mark Moore, "Violence Prevention: Criminal Justice or Public Health?" *Health Affairs,* vol. 12, no. 4, pp. 34–45.

103. Deborah Prothrow-Stith, quoted in Neil Hickey, "Violence on Television," *TV Guide,* 1992. See also Deborah Prothrow-Stith, with Michaele Weissman, *Deadly Consequences* (New York: HarperCollins, 1993).

PART III

1. Georg Büchner, *Danton's Death* (1835), tr. and adapted by James Maxwell (San Francisco: Chandler Publishing Company, 1961), p. 4.

2. Robert Bork, *Slouching Towards Gomorrah* (New York: HarperCollins, 1996), p. 140.

3. Nadine Strossen, *Defending Pornography* (New York: Doubleday, 1996), p. 42.

4. Williband Sauerlaender, "The Nazis' Theater of Seduction," *New York Review of Books,* April 21, 1994, p. 16.

5. Quoted by Newton N. Minow, in "Television's Values and the Values of Our Children" (Washington, D.C.: Annenberg Washington Program, 1995).

6. See Introduction for other arguments used to bring discussion of media violence to an end too abruptly.

7. Edward Gibbon, *Decline and Fall of the Roman Empire* (New York: Alfred A. Knopf, 1993), vol. 1, ch. 3, p. 76.

8. Juvenal, *Satires* VI, 1, 347. (Juvenal was speaking, however, of the guards guarding women, not of the office of censor.)

9. Blaise Pascal, *Penseés,* ch. 24, 60 (Paris: Classiques Garnier, 1991).

10. J. Bossuet, *Maximes et Réflexions sur la Comédie* (1694), in Ch. Urbain and E. Levesque, eds., *L'Eglise et le théâtre: Bossuet* (Paris: Bernard Grasset, 1930).

11. Ibid., p. 267. Bossuet attributed this practice to the Society of Jesus in his own time; others have pointed out that these rules had by then already been somewhat forgotten. See note 3 and references, same page.

12. Abbé de Saint-Pierre, "Mémoire pour rendre les Spectacles plus utiles à l'Etat," *Mercure de France,* April 1726.

13. Charles Desprez de Boissy, "Lettre sur les Spectacles" (1756), later added to and issued as *Lettres sur les Spectacles,* 4th ed. (Paris, 1771). The work was published anonymously, but the author's identity was known to most. See M. Barras, *Stage Controversy in France from Corneille to Rousseau* (1933; New York: Phaeton Press, 1977), pp. 245–49, for discussion.

14. Barras, *Stage Controversy,* p. 247.

15. Jean Le Rond d'Alembert, "Genève," in *L'Encyclopédie* (Lausanne and Berne, 1757), vol. 7, p. 578ff, tr. Allan Bloom in his edition of Jean-Jacques Rousseau, *Politics and the Arts: Letter to M. d'Alembert on the Theater* (Ithaca, N.Y.: Cornell University Press, 1960), appendix, p. 139.

16. Jean-Jacques Rousseau, *Lettre à M. D'Alembert sur les spectacles,* in *Oeuvres Complètes* (Paris: Gallimard, 1995), vol. 5, pp. 5, 31. My translation. See also Bloom tr., *Politics and the Arts,* pp. 5, 33–4.

17. Gibbon, in *The Decline and Fall of the Roman Empire,* could calmly hold that

although Rome had been vanquished by barbarians, "it may safely be presumed that no people, unless the face of nature is changed, will relapse into their original barbarism." (New York: Everyman's Library, 1954), p. 111.

18. During the previous summer, in 1757, Voltaire had been planning the next move in his campaign to be able to produce his plays and those of others without state or religious interference. When d'Alembert came to stay with Voltaire and to collect information for the article on Geneva he was preparing, the two discussed inserting a critique of the prohibition of all plays.

19. Jean Le Rond d'Alembert, "Discours préliminaire des éditeurs," in the *Encyclopédie, ou Dictionnaire raisonné des sciences, des arts at des métiers* (Paris: Briasson, David l'Aîné, Le Breton, Durand). Tr. Richard Schwab as *Preliminary Discourse to the Encyclopedia of Diderot* (Chicago: University of Chicago Press, 1995).

20. Voltaire, "Commentaires sur Corneille," quoted in Roger Pearson, *The Fables of Reason: A Study of Voltaire's "Contes Philosophiques"* (Oxford: Clarendon Press, 1993), p. 3.

21. See Richard Sennett, *The Fall of Public Man* (New York: W. W. Norton, 1974), pp. 115–22.

22. Rousseau, *Letter*, p. 24.

23. Ibid., p. 25.

24. Ibid., pp. 83, 91, 103.

25. The controversy also played a role in the official outlawing of further work on the *Encyclopedia*. D'Alembert resigned his editorship, leaving Diderot to struggle along to publish the remaining volumes.

26. When Gibbon spent some years in Lausanne, he was a frequent visitor to Voltaire's theatricals. See his accounts in Edward Gibbon, *Autobiography* (1796), ed. J. B. Bury (Oxford: Oxford University Press, 1978), pp. 80 and 132.

27. Voltaire, letter to d'Argental, quoted in Léon Fontaine, ed., J.-J. Rousseau, *Lettre à d'Alembert sur les spectacles* (Paris: Librairie Garnier Frères, 1889), p. 65.

28. Jean Le Rond d'Alembert, "Lettre à M. Rousseau, citoyen de Genève, par M. d'Alembert, de l'Académie Française," in Léon Fontaine, ed., *Lettre à d'Alembert sur les spectacles* (Paris: Librairie Garnier Frères, 1926), appendix 3, pp. 300–33.

29. Barras, *Stage Controversy*, p. 10.

30. Ong-Chew Peck Wan, letter, March 20, 1997 in response to my inquiry.

31. Ibid.

32. Ibid.

33. James Kynge, "Tough Rap Ahead on Ambitious Marathon in Singapore," *Financial Times*, February 18, 1997, p. 2.

34. Våldsskildringsrådet, *En handbok i fyra kapitel om våldsskildringar i våra medier* (Stockholm, Sweden: Department of Culture, 1995), p. 14.

35. Våldsskingringsrådet, Stockholm: *Flödet*, January 1996, p. 13.

36. See Leila Conners, "Freedom to Connect," *Wired,* August 1997, pp. 106–107.

37. Neil Postman, *Amusing Ourselves to Death* (New York: Penguin Books, 1986), p. 141.

38. *New York Times Co. v. United States,* 403 U.S. 713, 717 (1970).

39. See my "TV Violence, Children, and the Press: Eight Rationales Inhibiting Public Policy Debates" (Cambridge, Mass.: Joan Shorenstein Barone Center, April 1994), Discussion paper D-16.

40. C. Edwin Baker, "Advertising and a Democratic Press," *University of Pennsylvania Law Review,* vol. 140 (June 1992), pp. 2097–2243.

41. Birgitta Höjer, "Våldsskildringar i TV-Nyheter" (Stockholm: Vålds-skildringsrådet, 1995).

42. Bill Moyers, personal communication, March 1997.

43. "Unofficial Summary," United Nations Convention on the Rights of the Child, adopted by the United Nations on November 20, 1989.

44. See Laura M. Purdy, *In Their Best Interest? The Case Against Equal Rights for Children* (Ithaca, N.Y.: Cornell University Press, 1992), for a discussion of the libertarian view of the rights of children.

45. United Nations Convention, article 13.

46. See, for example, C. Edwin Baker, *Human Liberty and Freedom of Speech* (New York: Oxford University Press, 1989); Alexander Bickel, *The Morality of Consent* (New Haven: Yale University Press, 1975); Archibald Cox, *Freedom of Expression* (Cambridge, Mass.: Harvard University Press, 1981); Ronald Dworkin, *Taking Rights Seriously* (Harvard University Press, 1977); Thomas I. Emerson, *The System of Freedom of Expression* (New York: Random House, 1970); J.M. Goetzee, *Giving Offense: Essays on Censorship* (Chicago: University of Chicago Press, 1996); Kent Greenawalt, *Fighting Words: Individuals, Communities, and Liberties of Speech* (Princeton, N.J.: Princeton University Press, 1995); Gerald Gunther, *Cases and Materials on Individual Rights in Constitutional Law* (Mineola, N.Y.: Foundation Press, 1989); Anthony Lewis, *Make No Law* (New York: Random House, 1991); Rodney Smolla, *Free Speech in an Open Society* (New York: Alfred A. Knopf, 1992).

47. Catharine A. MacKinnon, "Pornography as Defamation and Discrimination," *Boston University Law Review,* 1991; Catharine A. MacKinnon, *Only Words* (Cambridge, Mass.: Harvard University Press, 1996); Deborah Rhode, *Justice and Gender: Sex Discrimination and the Law* (Cambridge, Mass.: Harvard University Press, 1989); *Speaking of Sex: The Denial of Gender Inequality* (Cambridge, Mass.: Harvard University Press, 1997); and Strossen, *Defending Pornography.*

48. *Reno v. American Civil Liberties Union et al.,* June 26, 1997.

49. Newton N. Minow and Craig L. LaMay, *Abandoned in the Wasteland: Children, Television, and the First Amendment* (New York: Hill and Wang, 1995), p. 136.

50. Cass Sunstein, *Democracy and the Problem of Free Speech* (New York: Free Press, 1993), p. xviii.

51. Cass Sunstein, *The Partial Constitution* (Cambridge, Mass.: Harvard University Press, 1990), p 221.

52. Rhode, *Justice and Gender*, p. 271.

53. Rhode, *Speaking of Sex*, pp. 137–38.

54. Kevin W. Saunders, *Violence as Obscenity: Limiting the Media's First Amendment Protection* (Durham, N.C.: Duke University Press, 1996), p. 3.

55. Ibid., ch. 1, 2.

56. *Miller v. California*, 413 U.S. 15, 1973.

57. Saunders, *Violence as Obscenity*, p. 134.

58. Ibid., p. 185.

59. Bork, *Slouching Towards Gomorrah*, p. 140.

60. Ibid., p. 153.

61. Ibid.

62. Harry T. Edwards and Mitchell N. Berman, "Regulating Violence on Television," *Northwestern University Law Review*, vol. 89, no. 4 (1995), pp. 1487–1566.

63. Ibid., p. 1492.

64. Ibid., pp. 1500, 1517–22.

65. Ibid., p. 1566.

66. A dilemma has been defined as "a situation where an agent has a *strong* moral obligation or requirement to adopt each of two alternatives, and neither is overridden, but the agent cannot adopt both alternatives." But the term dilemma is also used more broadly to signify any conflict presenting a choice between alternatives. See Walter Sinnott-Armstrong, "Moral Dilemma," *Cambridge Dictionary of Philosophy* (1995), p. 508; see also his *Moral Dilemmas* (Oxford: Basil Blackwell, 1988).

PART IV

1. William James, *Pragmatism* (1907; Cambridge, Mass.: Harvard University Press, 1975), p. 139.

2. See Part Two.

3. See, for example, Center for Media Literacy, at www.medialit.org.

4. Aristotle, *"Art" of Rhetoric*, 1355b tr. J. H. Friese (Cambridge, Mass.: Loeb Classical Library, Harvard University Press, 1975), p. 13.

5. For websites, see Center for Media Literacy: http://medialit.org/; Cultural Environment Movement: http://www.cemnet.org/; Mediascope: http://www.mediascope.org/; TV-Free America: http://www.essential.org/orgs/tvfa/; UNESCO International Clearinghouse on Children and Violence on the Screen, http://www.nordicom.gu.se/. For email addresses, see: National Alliance for Nonviolent Programming: NA4NVP@aol.com; and Parents' Choice: pchoice@erols.com.

6. Public Law no. 104–104, 1996, reinforcing the Children's Television Act of 1990.

7. Ibid., sections 551 (b) and (c).

8. *Reno v. American Civil Liberties Union et al.*, June 26, 1997.

9. Edward Donnerstein, "Mass Media Violence: Thoughts on the Debate," *Hofstra Law Review*, vol. 22 (1994), p. 831.

10. Ted Herbert, quoted in Ken Auletta, "What Won't They Do?", *New Yorker*, May 17, 1993, pp. 45–55, at 53.

11. Martha Minow and Richard Waistbourd, "Societal Movements for Children," *Daedalus*, Winter 1993, pp. 1–30, at 5. See also references in note 12, Part Two.

12. Newton N. Minow and Craig L. LaMay, *Abandoned in the Wasteland* (New York: Hill and Wang, 1995), p. 18.

13. Ibid.

14. Jerome Bruner, in *Acts of Meaning* (Cambridge, Mass.: Harvard University Press, 1990), p. 83, refers to studies of parents of disadvantaged children in the rural South who tell them stories of unusual violence with the express purpose of inuring them to life's hardships at an early age.

15. See Neil Anderson, *Media Works* (Oxford: Oxford University Press, 1989); and Madeline Levine, *Viewing Violence* (New York: Doubleday, 1996).

16. When *Schindler's List* was about to be broadcast on television, Spielberg was quoted as saying that the film was not, in his opinion, one that should be shown to the very young. His own children, of elementary school age, had not seen it in 1997; but he would want them to once they were of high school age. See Caryn James, "Bringing Home the Horror of the Holocaust," *New York Times*, February 23, 1997, p. 36 H.

17. Steven Spielberg, quoted by Stephen Schiff in "Seriously Spielberg," *New Yorker*, March 21, 1994, p. 101.

18. James Garbarino, *Raising Children in a Socially Toxic Environment* (San Francisco: Jossey-Bass, 1995), p. 163.

19. David Gonzalez, "Bishops Take on a 'Culture of Violence,'" *New York Times*, November 26, 1994, p. A11.

20. Kathleen Sullivan, personal communication.

21. James T. Hamilton, "Marketing Violence: The Impact of Labeling Violent Television Content," Working Paper, Terry Sanford Institute of Public Policy, Duke University, 1995. See also James T. Hamilton, *Channeling Violence: The Economic Market for Violent Television Programming* (Princeton, N.J.: Princeton University Press, 1998).

22. Walter Goodman, *New York Times*, "TV Violence: A Solution with Risks." August 9, 1995, p. C14.

23. David Lange, Robert K. Baker, and Sandra J. Ball, *Mass Media and Violence*, vol. 11 of *A Report to the National Commission on the Causes and Prevention of Violence* (Washington, D.C.: U.S. Government Printing Office, 1969), pp. 359, 378–79.

24. American Academy of Pediatrics, "Children, Adolescents, and Television," *Pediatrics*, vol. 96, no. 4 (October 1995), pp. 786–87.

25. Bill Bradley, quoted by Jim Sleeper in "Two Worlds Collide on the Levin Death," *Boston Globe*, June 11, 1997, p. A27.

26. The criteria for what constitutes quality educational television, however, have often been very loosely defined.

27. Peggy Charren, personal communication.

28. Canadian Radio-television and Telecommunications Commission, "Canada and TV Violence: Cooperation and Consensus," 1995.

29. For an outline of measures taken, beginning early in 1990, by the Canadian Radio-television and Telecommunications Commission, see CRTC Fact Sheet, TV1-10-93: CRTC Initiatives Regarding Violence on Television.

30. Canadian Radio-television and Telecommunications Commission, "Voluntary Code Regarding Violence in Television Programming," Public Notice CRTC 1993-149, Ottawa, October 28, 1993.

31. Keith Spicer, quoted in *Respecting Children: A Canadian Agenda for Children's Television* (Ottawa: CRTC, 1996).

32. Norwegian Ministry of Cultural Affairs, "The Norwegian Government's Campaign to Combat violence in the Visual Media" (Oslo, 1993).

33. Ibid., p. 5.

34. Ibid., p. 14.

35. Ibid., p. 6.

36. Jostein Gripsrud, "La Mort de Silje: Les médias sont-ils responsables?" *Les Cahiers de la Sécurité Intéerieure*, no. 20, 1995, pp. 70–76.

37. Mohandas Gandhi, quoted by Arun Gandhi, personal correspondence. See also Arun Gandhi, ed., *World Without Violence: Can Gandhi's Vision Become Reality?* (New Delhi: Wiley Eastern Ltd., 1994).

ACKNOWLEDGMENTS

I would like to thank four research centers for support, research assistance, and most congenial fellowship and debates during the years when I was preparing this book: The Center for Advanced Study in the Behavioral Sciences, in Stanford, California; The Joan Shorenstein Barone Center for the Press, Politics, and Public Policy, at Harvard University; The Annenberg Washington Program; and the Harvard Center for Population and Development Studies. I am happy to thank the friends and colleagues whose advice I've been able to draw upon in writing this book; and to thank, in particular, those who were kind enough to offer their comments after reading all or parts of it: Bruce Knauft, Kathleen Coleman, Ellen Hume, Jennifer Leaning, Zeph Stewart, Barbara Ursel, and Berit Griebenow. I am grateful to Ellen Goodman and Robert Levey for proposing the book's present title as an alternative to its tedious working title. I count myself fortunate to have been able to rely, once again, on the wise counsel and expertise of a superb editor, Merloyd Lawrence. For their scrupulous and most helpful attention to the manuscript, I thank the copy editor, Janet Biehl, and the production manager, Tiffany Cobb. My special thanks go to my children, Hilary, Victoria, and Tomas, along with my husband Derek, for their kindness, interest, and support throughout, coupled with unsparing and utterly indispensable critiques of successive drafts. To my grandson, finally, born as the manuscript was going into production, this book is lovingly dedicated.

INDEX

ABOUT THE AUTHOR

Sissela Bok was born in Sweden and educated in Switzerland, France, and the United States. She received a Ph.D. in philosophy from Harvard University in 1970. She has been professor of Philosophy at Brandeis University and a fellow at the Shorenstein Barone Center for Press, Politics, and Public Policy at the John F. Kennedy School of Government at Harvard University. Now Distinguished Fellow at the Harvard Center for Population and Development Studies, she frequently comments on ethical issues in government, media, and public life. Her books include *Lying: Moral Choice in Public and Private Life; Secrets: On the Ethics of Concealment and Revelation; Alva Myrdal: A Daughter's Memoir* and *Common Values.*